Risky Business

Risky Business

Why Leaders Must Develop a Disruptive Mindset

Linda Henman, Ph.D.

Routledge
Taylor & Francis Group

A PRODUCTIVITY PRESS BOOK

First published 2021 by
Routledge
600 Broken Sound Parkway #300, Boca Raton FL, 33487

and by Routledge
2 Park Square, Milton Park, Abingdon, Oxon OX14 4RN

Routledge is an imprint of the Taylor & Francis Group, an informa business

© 2021 Linda Henman

ISBN: 9780367768157 (hbk)
ISBN: 9780367768171 (pbk)
ISBN: 9781003168669 (ebk)

Typeset in Minion
by Newgen Publishing UK

For Mark Witman,

a wellspring of talent, insight, support, and affection.

Contents

Foreword

Stop! Don't do it. Don't make that decision yet, at least not before you have heard what Dr. Linda Henman has to say.

Decision-making is a risky business, in large part because we have been conditioned to trust our brain, our inner voice, and our gut instinct. And yet, as Linda points out in *Risky Business*, the brain is lazy, habitual, in search of shortcuts, and quite frankly, not to be trusted.

We take our brain for granted; we assume we are making good decisions; and without realizing we are doing it, we draw constantly on mental models we already have stored away in order to calculate the risk of the decisions we are about to make. What we often do not recognize is that we limit our creativity because of the habitual search for familiarity, pattern recognition, confirmation bias, and what I call "I have seen this before and I know it works" syndrome.

Linda takes us on a historical journey, exploring different experts, different mental models, and different viewpoints on how unconscious bias impacts the quality of our decision-making processes. She speaks of the need to examine our beliefs and move them from being unconscious to conscious. Not impossible, and yet, easier said than done.

We first need to become aware of the beliefs driving our decisions. We need to honestly explore the impact of these beliefs and then move them from the back of our necks to the edge of our shoulders. My research indicates that we cannot ever fully get rid of our unconscious biases, but we can become much better at noticing them and intervening before they negatively impact decision-making.

The 2018 Gallop Poll on Employee Engagement found that only 34% of people are engaged at work; 66% are disengaged; and 13% of them are actively disengaged and described as "sleeping on the job." We ask people to bring their best selves to work, to be innovative and creative and yet, how can that happen when we are downloading old programming, preconceived patterns, and biases? What impact does our lazy habitual brain have on critical business decisions, including hiring practices, promotion prospects, or working on anti-racism initiatives within organizations?

One of my psychology professors once said, "There is no such thing as the innocent eye." We are not as objective as we think we are—we see the world through the lens of our subjectivity. In other words, we filter our objectivity through our own subjectivity and social construction. Stephen Covey said that we see the world as *we* are, not as *it* is. If all of that is true, it makes our decisions less stable and conceivably more impulsive. How can we guard against believing we are making logical, fair-minded business decisions, when in fact we are not?

Linda talks about high-stakes decisions and the need to close the gap between what we say and what we actually do. I would add that the challenge begins much sooner. It is imperative that we *first* explore what we are *thinking* before anything comes out of our mouths. For example, I am guessing that most people think of themselves as a well-intentioned individual, making objective, logical, fair-minded business decisions and doing all of that while being a diversity sensitive and inclusive leader. Yet, many of our decisions are not logical at all and are influenced by things we are not consciously aware of. For example, a recent study of leaders on a pre-employment interview panel found that they had different perceptions of candidates based on *what they were holding in their hands*! If the interviewers held a hot beverage rather than an ice-cold drink, they were more likely to perceive the candidate warmly.

Linda points out that

> High-stakes decisions demand that we close the gap between what we *say* and what we actually *do*—the intersection of what we believe and how we behave. Then we can begin to understand how our unconscious beliefs create biases that shape our world view—and our mindset.

Results from *Cognizant,* my unconscious bias online assessment, indicate that what we believe and how we behave do indeed produce different results.

I encourage the reader to take a deep dive into *Risky Business* and to explore both conscious and unconscious decision-makings more fully to understand their impact on the day-to-day decisions we make, both at work and at home. I contend that we will never *not* be biased, but we can understand the biases we have, how they show up, and what we can do to mitigate them. *Risky Business* sets out a roadmap for doing just that.

Helen Turnbull, Ph.D., CSP & Global Speaking Fellow
Author of The Illusion of Inclusion

Introduction

More than a hundred years ago, Freud noted our natural fascination with individuals of extraordinary talent, achievement, and power. According to him, we feel drawn by their glamour and curious about the special abilities that make it possible, indeed essential, for them to enact upon the public stage the hopes and dreams we all possess but fear to carry out ourselves. We follow with great interest the fortunes and decisions these leaders make, often second-guessing their decisions but more often fascinated by the risks they willingly embrace.

More recent research tells us that in the average person's stream of consciousness, most of us devote about 12% of our daily thoughts to the future. I find that number suspiciously low, but even at 12%, that means, during an average eight-hour workday, a typical person spends an hour thinking about things that have yet to happen. The past helps us predict the future—but not very accurately. Why do our beliefs, thoughts, and emotions insist on projecting us into an unknown and perhaps precarious future? Flip a three-sided coin. Some of us will land on the side of the risk reluctant; others will find themselves risk tolerant; but some will land on another side—living among the risk enthusiasts. In all three cases, the person's mindset determines the outcome.

For more than 20 years, I have aggregated data from the assessments of Disruptive Leaders™ who have reached the level of vice president or higher in my client companies, with companies in five industries represented. On the abstract thinking and risk-taking measures, the leaders in my study scored in the *above*-average range. On the impulsivity scale, they scored well *below* average—indicating many of the myths and stereotypes we have about effective leadership simply aren't true.

As exceptional abstract thinkers, these Disruptive Leaders eagerly engage in long-range strategic planning, simultaneously process information from a variety of sources, and deal with multi-dimensional issues. They like to gamble because they feel stimulated by the process of putting the pieces of a puzzle together that no one else has ever put together before. They derive great satisfaction from a strategy that pays, an M & A deal that makes money immediately after the deal closes, and dramatic growth. They take risks not *in spite* of the element of the unknown but *because* of it.

Here's what else I've learned. People don't necessarily understand their own mindset, and they have even worse luck understanding the mindsets of others. When faced with a make-or-break decision, people *demonstrate* the kind of mindset they possess. The way people handle risk and crisis often telegraphs what is happening between their two ears.

Risk-reluctant people dread failure. They see it as a testament to their inabilities, questionable intelligence, and dubious integrity. Those who can engage in risky business, however, don't mind or fear failure as much because they realize they learn from it. This book explains that, with the right mindset, you can motivate yourself and those you lead, teach, and love to transform their lives and your own for the better.

Our instincts and risk-aversion conspire to make us perceive the world as a scary place, a place where we probably shouldn't even do business. The problem? We don't know what we don't know, and unconscious, predictable biases and fear inform our guesses and our behavior—and stand in the way of us engaging in *Risky Business*.

Our fears, perceptions, and biases tell one story, but the facts tell another. The world, for all its imperfections, is in better shape than we might think, even in our COVID-confused climate. We have real problems, but when we spend our energies worrying about the future or feeling guilty about the past, we lose focus and exhaust our abilities to solve problems, make high-caliber decisions, and take the necessary risks to grow and change.

When our intellect and our emotions wage war, resilience and motivation suffer the consequences—the victims of a situation they didn't want in the first place. When this happens, we start to alter our beliefs, often developing a victim mentality, one characterized by pessimism and despair. How can a person tolerate ambiguity with such a mindset?

Revolutionary ideas constantly besiege leaders, and individuals can have a major impact on history but *only if they are willing to take a chance on their ideas*. It won't happen automatically. Five psychological forces influence high-stakes decision-making: beliefs, cognition, emotions, motivation, and resilience. When we embody all five, we develop a Disruptive Mindset™. We don't ignore, diminish, or deny fear; we accept it. We trust our abilities to sail in unchartered seas.

As systemic, discerning *thinkers*, we commit ourselves to continuous learning and consistently remain open to new ideas without being naïve— all the while avoiding the trap of hubris. But we also need to understand how we *feel*, how human emotions function, and the psychology behind risk-taking. Then, with optimism and a commitment to excellence, we can steadfastly move ideas to action.

A Disruptive Mindset—one that shapes resilience—recognizes that challenges aren't permanent; talented people can figure out problems; and even failure isn't fatal. This mindset allows us to learn from past mistakes, so we can move past them and thrive. Taxi drivers didn't create Uber; horse breeders didn't start the Ford Motor Company; AT&T didn't invent the iPhone; and Macy's didn't found Amazon. Leaders with a Disruptive Mindset did.

Benjamin R. Barber, American political theorist and author, said, "I don't divide the world into the weak and the strong, or the successes and the failures, those who make it or those who don't. I divide the world into learners and non-learners." *Risky Business* examines learning and explains what we must do to create disruption so we can prepare ourselves for success. That can happen only when we learn how to innovate rapidly for maximum gain within tolerable risk parameters. This enables us to create a culture of innovative behavior to foster new ideas for market dominance— and feelings of personal mastery.

Growth, change, and disruption exist for their own reasons. Most of us have presumed, assumed, subsumed, and sometimes submerged the links between volatility and improvement. That doesn't have to happen. By examining existing research and aggregating new information, we can understand how to overcome what author James O'Toole aptly characterized as "the ideology of comfort and the tyranny of custom."

1

The Disruptive Mindset

Let's start with a brief history lesson. The military draft in the U.S. ended in 1973 at the conclusion of the Vietnam War. At that time, the U.S. moved to an all-volunteer armed service. Fast forward five years to 1978 when I began my consulting career, with the U.S. Air Force as my first client. In 1978, my friend, then Capt. Emily Chamberlin, hired me to develop training programs for Social Actions, a division within The Twelfth Air Force at Bergstrom Air Force Base. Social Actions existed to support the non-technical aspects of military life. The division often addressed this directive by offering mandatory training programs on various aspects of social justice. Social Actions training days were even *less* popular than flu-shot days.

Emily hired me because senior Air Force leaders of the Tactical Air Command realized they would need new approaches when they introduced women into functions women had not held before. They intended these programs to make the transition easier for both the leaders *and* the women. Emily and I thought it would make sense to test our training by delivering it to eight of the most senior sergeants in the Air Force to get their feedback.

Picture this: At age 27, I walk into a room of eight men, roughly the age of my father. They have so many stripes on their sleeves, I get vertigo. I see these stripes because all eight men have their arms folded across their chests, the question on their faces unmistakable: "*Honey*, what have *you* got to teach *us*?" No one talked about either mindset or disruption in 1978, but if they had, these eight men would have initially personified the *opposite* of a Disruptive Mindset. But that changed in the span of six hours.

Keep in mind, at 27 I had absolutely no qualifications, at least in their minds, to facilitate a discussion about the role of women in the future of

5

the Air Force. I had never led anything other than the prom committee, and I had never served in uniform.

On that day in 1978 I had two epiphanies simultaneously: (1) these Chief Master Sergeants had forgotten more than I'd ever know about leadership, and (2) I needed to honor and leverage the wisdom in the room. We had a successful day, and the story has a happy ending. Together we developed some successful approaches those leaders and others who came after them in the Tactical Air Command implemented for years.

Emily, the Chiefs, and I didn't know we had collectively formed a Disruptive Mindset, but we had. We challenged what we'd always believed, leveraged our smarts, put egos aside, steadfastly kept our eyes on the goal, and emerged from the experience ready to tackle all the challenges that would come as a result of our work that day. Although no one used the term "mindset," we collectively demonstrated a "can-do attitude."

Since that day, I've learned a great deal more about leadership, mindset, risk, and disruption, but I've never had a day when I learned so much at once. My instant education would not have been possible but for the willingness of everyone to explore uncharted seas. We all felt curious about what it would take to make the Air Force's transition successful, willing to at least *tolerate* ambiguity, and, in general, keen to figure out how to make this disruption work.

WHAT DOES "MINDSET" MEAN?

In 2006, after decades of research, Stanford University psychologist Carol Dweck, Ph.D., introduced a simple but revolutionary idea: the power of mindset. Her research indicated that how we think about our talents and abilities determines our success in every human endeavor—school, work, sports, the arts, and business. In her groundbreaking book, *Mindset: The New Psychology of Success*, Dweck noted that people with a *fixed mindset*—those who believe that abilities are permanent—flourish less often than those with a *growth mindset*—those who believe they can develop abilities.

Others since Dweck have introduced the terms "poverty mindset," and "scarcity mindset." Poverty mentality influences behaviors consistent with beliefs that money shouldn't be spent; we have limited opportunities; risk brings too much danger; success is temporary and non-replicable; and generally remaining in the back of the pack is safest. This sort of scarcity mindset tells us there will never be enough, so we must steadfastly guard what we have.

Conversely, an "abundance mindset" assures us we can attain and replicate success. We will always have enough, so we can afford to take risks. We have the talents to handle most situations we encounter successfully. (And in those times when we can't, we will be resilient enough to bounce back quickly.)

Dweck offered a simple but revolutionary view of achievement: how we see our intelligence, personality, and talent influences how we learn, work, live, love, and succeed or fail in life. She also exhibited what I call a *Disruptive Mindset*, but, like most others who have demonstrated a disruptive orientation, she had her fault finders.

Critics pointed out that no one could replicate her research—a key requirement for scientific validity. University of Edinburgh psychology professor Timothy Bates commented that a claim that personal effort entirely dictates performance in a cognitive task flies in the face of more than 100 years of intelligence research. Other critics from the fields of education and psychology expressed concern that considering mindset as a psychological construct would lead educators to assess and grade *attitudes* in children, and, by extension, we might be tempted to start evaluating general performance on attitudes rather than observable behavior.

In 2005, David Geary introduced *The Origin of Mind: Evolution of Brain, Cognition, and General Intelligence*. In this work, the author discussed Charles Darwin's opinion that understanding the evolution of the human mind and brain stands at the heart of evolutionary sciences. Geary drew from Darwin's observations to propose an integrated theory of why and how the human mind has developed to function as it does. He posited that human motivation, emotional, behavioral, and cognitive systems have evolved to process social and ecological information. He further argued that the ultimate focus of all these systems is to support our attempts to gain access to and control of resources—the social, biological, and physical resources that support survival.

Who's right? Today most experts agree that the conventional "nature or nurture" questions don't really help us understand human behavior. We now know that our genes and the environment cooperate as we develop. However, we also now understand that we have more capacity for lifelong learning and brain development than we previously imagined. More than

100 years ago, Alfred Binet, the French psychologist who developed the first practical IQ test, noted that the people who start out the smartest don't end up the smartest. To my knowledge, Binet never used the word "mindset," but his writing suggests he understood the concept a century ago.

When we wrote *The Merger Mindset: How to Get it Right in the High-Stakes World of Mergers, Acquisitions, and Divestitures*, my coauthor, psychologist Dr. Constance Dierickx, and I concluded that the view you adopt for yourself profoundly affects the way you lead your life—and how you engage in high-stakes decision-making.

Drawing from Dr. Dweck's work, we explored how believing that a *fixed mindset*—one that tells us our talents and qualities resist change—creates an urgency to prove ourselves over and over. This kind of mindset erects roadblocks to our success and keeps us in a constant, confusing spiral. We see our gifts—or the lack thereof—as the hand we were dealt and must live with.

Conversely, a *growth mindset* causes us to believe that the hand we're dealt is just the starting point for development. We view our talents as attributes we can cultivate through our efforts and strategies. Although people may differ in every significant way—in their initial talents, aptitudes, and temperaments—everyone can change and grow through application and experience. Dweck asked, "Do people with this mindset believe that anyone can be anything, that anyone with proper motivation or education can become Einstein or Beethoven?" No, but they believe a person's true potential remains unknown (and unknowable) and that no one can foresee what an individual can accomplish with years of passion, toil, and training.

Many of the people we now consider shining stars were once considered dull. High school coaches once cut professional athletes we now deem "great" from the JV team. Teachers once thought Darwin and Tolstoy were ordinary children. Ben Hogan, one of the greatest golfers of all time, appeared completely uncoordinated and graceless as a child. Acting instructors routinely advised today's stars to give up on acting careers. However, these "greats" had a growth mindset that allowed them to overcome their weaknesses and ignore the wrong-headed advice of their coaches and critics. In other words, the people with the growth mindset were amazingly accurate, and those with a fixed mindset were wrong.[1] The passion for stretching oneself and sticking to it even, or especially, when the going gets tough is the hallmark of the growth mindset.

Baseball fans regard Babe Ruth as one of the greatest sports heroes of all time, primarily because of his hitting record. However, at the beginning of his career, Ruth performed as a powerful-but-inconsistent hitter. As a pitcher, no one really expected Ruth to do great things at bat, so he began experimenting, and more importantly, he developed a systematic, disciplined approach to his hitting. With his abdomen bulging out of his Yankee uniform, few would have characterized Ruth as a "natural," yet we remember him for the records he set through dogged determination.

People with a growth mindset see failure as a setback—an opportunity to problem-solve—not as a direct hit on their self-esteem. They put things in perspective by realizing that if they never fail, they probably aren't playing in a challenging enough league. Those with a fixed mindset try to avoid doing anything that might expose their limitations.

When I was in elementary school, we often heard the threat, "This will go on your *permanent record.*" We reacted as though someone in the celestial kingdom had an accounting system that would follow us through life, dutifully recording the pluses and minuses of every school experience. It's no wonder so many of us developed a fixed mindset! If it's in the permanent record, there's no hope for changing it, whatever "it" happens to be.

Those with a fixed mindset never fulfill their potential because they fear failure—and even success—because they see both as entries into their permanent record. Now we know no permanent record follows us through life begging for crumbs, but many act as if one still exists. Otherwise, they would have the capacity to develop a Disruptive Mindset.

WHAT QUALIFIES AS A *DISRUPTIVE MINDSET*?

At the end of 2019, using the principles of the late management guru Peter Drucker, *The Wall Street Journal* announced its picks for the best-managed companies of the year. From 820 companies, Amazon.com Inc. took first place, and Microsoft rose to the number two position, followed by Apple Inc. in third place. A team of researchers compiled the list using dozens of data points to evaluate companies on five performance dimensions: customer satisfaction, employee engagement and development, innovation, social responsibility, and financial strength.

The performance dimensions describe these top-ranking companies, but they do more. They give us a glimpse into the mindset decision makers shared. That is, we can infer that senior leaders and board directors held some common beliefs about what success looks like and had the requisite talents, skills, and confidence to get the results they wanted.

We can also conclude that an unprecedented number of challenges continue to differentiate leaders who embody a Disruptive Mindset from their competitors who don't. At the same time, we can extrapolate that the way we have traditionally assessed an organization's ability to grow through innovation and transformation is outdated.

When Jeff Bezos founded Amazon, he didn't assemble retail experts to advise him about how to do something no one had done before. Taxi drivers didn't start Uber, and horse breeders didn't start the Ford Motor Company. Rather, these successful companies exist because of innovative solutions that came from those with Disruptive Mindsets.

Amazon catapulted to the top of the 2019 list by earning an off-the-charts ranking in innovation. Its score in that dimension of performance is more than double that of any other company. Amazon outpaces others in patent applications, trademark registrations, and spending on research and development. Amazon also abandons patent applications at a higher rate than others, a sign of its commitment to move past obsolete technology.

Bezos has long shunned lengthy slide presentations. Instead, employees present a memo that may not be longer than six pages. Everyone reads it prior to starting a meeting. Bezos praised the memo process in one of his letters to investors: "Some have the clarity of angels singing."[2] This succinct summary sets up the meeting for high-quality discussions, a fast pace, and agility—the opposite effect of cumbersome PowerPoint presentations in most other organizations.

Disruption alone doesn't create growth. Instead, growth creates disruption. Disruption for the sake of disruption would earn a low-ranking score among the companies *The Wall Street Journal* evaluated. For instance, Facebook Inc. received a low score on customer satisfaction, a score based on customers' unwillingness to recommend Facebook to a colleague or friend. "Borat" star, Sacha Baron Cohen, attacked Mark Zuckerberg in a speech in November 2019 at the Anti-Defamation League's International Leadership Summit, saying the social media giant's resistance to fact-checking ads relies on "twisted logic" that would have had it selling spots to Nazis in another generation. Many would argue Facebook experienced its share of disruption in 2019, but that disruption led to a sullied reputation, not growth and admiration.

A Disruptive Mindset involves more than innovation, cutting-edge technology, pace, and risk-taking—but they help. Disruption can happen slowly and methodically, causing so little discomfort that few would choose the word "disruptive" to describe the transformation. More often, however, disruption shows up dragging a breathless sense of urgency—if not crisis—with it.

When Constance Dierickx and I wrote *The Merger Mindset*, we built on Dweck's research but tailored the concept to apply to high-stakes deals, like mergers and acquisitions. We drew on our 60-plus years of collective experience helping leaders make the pivotal decisions that led to their success. We noticed these leaders had five things in common: a strong belief in themselves, the requisite intellectual horsepower, fortitude, motivation, and resilience (see Figure 1.1).

We thought of mindset as an internal monologue—the intrapersonal communication messages people send and receive within themselves. When we used the term *merger mindset*, we wanted to describe the frame of mind decision makers require.

FIGURE 1.1
Mindset Constructs.

From these beginnings sprang the notion of a Disruptive Mindset. I contrast a Disruptive Mindset to a stagnant one. Like its "fixed mindset" counterpart, a stagnant mindset causes us to see *effort* as bad—something that sets us up for failure. This way of thinking—or more accurately *not* thinking—stalls our growth because it causes us to prove constantly we're smart or talented. It validates and protects what we *have* instead of challenging us to get better.

A stagnant mindset often manifests itself in people who lack confidence or self-esteem. Similarly, when we observe narcissistic behavior, we witness someone who is self-protecting. These people seem self-aggrandizing, but in reality, their hypersensitive nature won't allow them to admit they're wrong. Of course, not everyone with a stagnant mindset has a personality disorder. Often, however, they avoid taking risks because they fear the guilt, doubt, and disappointment those risks may bring.

Those with a Disruptive Mindset demonstrate the opposite behavior. They see effort itself as good because it causes them to get smarter as they learn from mistakes. They remain open to accurate information, and they pursue learning. They believe they can grow their talent, and they love challenges. Resilient in the face of setbacks, they eagerly overcome adversity, always believing in the possibility of greater success. They accept what they can't change but remain clear about reality. They know they can't make themselves taller, but they constantly question how they can raise their stature with smarts and skills. They leverage strengths and live their beliefs.

Writers and theorists have described a mindset that interferes with our willingness to disrupt the status quo in several ways: fixed, poverty, victim, scarcity, or stagnant. While the terms vary and definitions change, often we see differences without distinctions. What, then, can we conclude about a mindset that interferes with disruption, change, and success?

- These people believe they are victims of circumstances. This belief, above all others, foreshadows a life of seeing themselves as powerless to change their lot in life. They feel as though the decisions and choices of others define their destinies. Often, they blame their parents or ancestors. Other times, they blame society, the government, or "them." Things can't change, and they focus on what they *don't* have and think they can't get.
- No commitment to change, personal development, education, or goal attainment exists. The most successful people I know do the

opposite. Each year, these people make a conscious effort to improve. They take a class, attend a conference, read books, or sign up for golf lessons. They enjoy their current situation immensely and still strive to improve their lives.

- By constantly comparing themselves to others, people with a scarcity mindset envy the "haves" and simultaneously feel guilty about having more than others. They allow others to set the temperature in the room instead of deciding for themselves what feels best.
- Those with a poverty mindset fear spending money on non-essentials. Their obsession with money leads to a constant search for the cheapest alternative, the best deal, the biggest discount, a free lunch, a get-rich-quick scheme, or *something for nothing*.
- Similarly, those with a scarcity mindset deny themselves luxuries they can afford like a nice dinner, a first-class airline ticket, a good bottle of wine, or other expensive objects they can well afford.
- A fixed mindset causes people to believe they're *lucky* when they succeed and incompetent when they fail. They imagine that good fortune plays an exaggerated role in their lives. They weren't the ones sitting at a traffic light who got rear-ended by a drunk driver or the ones who developed an illness. Consequently, they credit chance for their fate and fail to recognize their own efforts when they succeed.

HOW DO WE DEVELOP A DISRUPTIVE MINDSET?

The Matthew Effect is a social phenomenon often linked to the idea that the rich get richer and the poor get poorer. This refers to a common concept that those who already have status find themselves in situations where they gain more, and those who do not have prestige typically struggle to achieve more. The Matthew Effect also helps explain why some can embrace a disruptive, risk-taking mindset more readily than others can.

In 1968, sociologist Robert Merton used the term "The Matthew Effect" to explain the origins of exceptional people when he formulated the theory of "cumulative advantage." The term has its foundation in the Christian gospel of Matthew: "For to all those who have, more will be given, and they will have an abundance; but from those who have nothing, even what they have *will be taken away*." Merton used the term to describe how, among other things, eminent scientists often received more credit than a comparatively unknown researcher, even one who did similar work.

In educational circles, teachers started to use The Matthew Effect to explain why, in school, the rich get richer and the poor get poorer. That is, when children fail at reading, they begin to dislike reading. They read less than their classmates who read well. Consequently, these children do not gain vocabulary, background knowledge, and information. In short, the word-rich get richer, while the word-poor get poorer.

Successful people seem to engender more success. Superlative students get the finest teachers. The most gifted athletes receive the best coaching. If Beethoven had been born in the wilds of Africa, with no piano in sight, this accident of birth might have robbed civilization of one of the great musical geniuses of all time. Similarly, if Michelangelo's family had owned a bakery instead of a marble quarry, perhaps we'd now have a world-class torte that bore his signature instead of the Sistine Chapel. But none of this paints a credible picture of how those with a Disruptive Mindset come to walk among us.

For my book *Challenge the Ordinary*, I interviewed former Space Shuttle Commander and retired United Space Alliance CEO Dick Covey. Covey, a former Air Force "brat," had no special advantages in his childhood, such as private schooling or tutoring. Rather, like most military kids, he attended whatever school happened to be where the Air Force happened to send his dad—some good, some not quite so good.

Although advanced in his studies, no teacher would have called him a "good student"—but not because he couldn't learn. On the contrary, teachers found him challenging because he learned so fast he quickly became bored with the pedestrian pace of his high school classes in Northwest Florida. He did have direction and focus, however. He had read everything written about Alan Shepherd and knew he wanted to be an astronaut.

At the suggestion of his father's friend, Covey applied to and was accepted by the Air Force Academy. When he entered in 1964, he immediately enrolled in an accelerated math and science program to prepare him for eventual graduate work at Purdue in astronautical and aeronautical engineering. Had he not enrolled in this program immediately after entering the Academy, he would not have qualified. From an early age, he received and heeded sound advice, and he constantly thought ahead.

Covey received a master's degree in seven months and then began undergraduate pilot training in March 1969. Even though he had never flown and had to compete with scores of those who had, he graduated first in his class for academics and second overall, behind a student who entered pilot training with 1,700 hours. After graduation, he took more training to learn to fly three fighters in as many years.

After completing 339 combat missions in Southeast Asia and accumulating more than a thousand hours of flight time, Covey applied to test pilot school—the path he had determined would lead him to the Astronaut Corps. His dreams came to fruition when NASA selected him from thousands of applicants to fill one of 15 slots.

Covey demonstrates that those who learn quickly, give others reason to trust them, and exhibit strong character overcome the major hurdles that impede the advancement of those who never become top performers. But that explains only part of the reason he developed a Disruptive Mindset. Covey had some of the elements of cumulative advantage. He was born with intelligence; his father had smart friends who could give him sage advice; and he was the right gender (in his era, only males were allowed into the Air Force Academy, fighter squadrons, and NASA).

When botanists find a rare orchid, they scrutinize the characteristics of the superior seed and then research the environmental constructs that led to the exquisite flower: soil conditions, weather, temperature, moisture, etc. Similarly, when we encounter the human equivalent, we should examine the salient factors that led to the development of the virtuoso.

Nature or nurture? The answer doesn't matter. Covey's high school teachers may have found him challenging, but I doubt many found his success surprising. He identified an objective, listened to wise counsel, delayed reward, and then committed himself to those who would develop his greatness. Does the credit for a bumper crop go to the plant or to the farmer? Probably both.

So, what if you've spent your entire life with a stagnant mindset—one that has kept you from taking risks and challenging assumptions about yourself? Can people develop or adopt a Disruptive Mindset in adulthood after decades of seeing themselves with limitations? Absolutely. The chapters that follow will outline specific actions you can take, but here's a quick summary:

1. Become self-aware. Challenge long-held assumptions about yourself, others, and the world around you. Seek trusted advisors who will help you know yourself better.

2. Develop skills and abilities that will give you the confidence you'll need to take risks.
3. Self-regulate. Don't let emotional reactions define you.
4. Stay motivated by rewarding yourself for effort, not just goal accomplishment.
5. Bounce back from setbacks. Wallowing in self-pity does no one any good.

WHAT ABOUT AMBIGUITY TOLERANCE?

In her 2001 bestseller *Seabiscuit*, author Laura Hillenbrand introduced readers to an underdog story about the horse who came out of nowhere to become a legend. Seabiscuit, a small horse so broken that owners had considered euthanizing him, stood only 15 hands high. This smallish mud-colored animal with forelegs that didn't straighten all the way had an inauspicious start to his racing career, winning only one-fourth of his first 40 races. Yet, he became an unlikely champion and a symbol of hope to many Americans during the Great Depression.

Seabiscuit out ran the 1937 Triple-Crown winner, and fans voted him American Horse of the Year for 1938. He went on to become one of the most electrifying and popular attractions in sports history and the single biggest newsmaker in the world in 1938, receiving more coverage than FDR, Hitler, or Mussolini! The little horse became the top money-winning racehorse up to the 1940s. His success came as a surprise to the racing establishment, which had written off the crooked-legged racehorse with the sad tail and tale.

Three men with Disruptive Mindsets changed the damaged horse and the course of horse-racing history. With hindsight, we might also consider Seabiscuit's whole team of people—the jockey, the owner, the trainer—damaged in one way or another, too.

Red Pollard, the jockey whom many considered too big to ride a little horse, lost vision in his right eye early in his career. The accident happened because of a traumatic brain injury Pollard suffered when he was hit in the head by a rock thrown up by another horse during a training ride. Because he would not have been allowed to ride had the full extent of his injury been known, he kept his vision loss a secret for the rest of his riding career.

Born in a log cabin in the backwoods of northwest Georgia, Tom Smith, Seabiscuit's trainer, came from humble beginnings. Hillenbrand described Smith as the mysterious, virtually mute mustang breaker, a refugee from the vanishing frontier.

Seabiscuit's owner, Charles Stewart Howard, began his career as a bicycle mechanic but made his fortune as an automobile dealer. After overcoming tragedy in his personal life, he went on to establish himself as a successful owner of thoroughbred horses.

Through their dogged determination and against all odds, these three men disrupted themselves into winners. A down-and-out nation saw this horse and his rider as a symbol of what a team could accomplish through grit, spirit, and unorthodox training methods. Over four years, these unlikely partners survived a phenomenal run of bad luck to transform Seabiscuit from a pathetic glue-factory candidate into an American sports icon.[3]

Nine years after the success with *Seabiscuit*, Laura Hillenbrand wrote another bestseller *Unbroken*. She recounted, on a May afternoon in 1943, an Army Air Force bomber crashed into the Pacific Ocean and disappeared, leaving only a spray of debris and a slick of oil, gasoline, and blood—and leaving a young lieutenant, Louis Zamperini, the plane's bombardier, stranded in a life raft. So began one of the most extraordinary odysseys of World War II.

In his early years, Zamperini had been a sneaky and incorrigible delinquent, often breaking into houses, fighting, and fleeing his home to ride the rails. He changed in his teens, however. He began to channel his defiance into running, discovering an extraordinary talent that carried him to the Berlin Olympics and within reach of the four-minute mile. But when the world war came, the athlete became an airman, beginning a journey that would lead to his doomed flight and a personal war against the elements.

Zamperini survived the crash of the plane, but ahead lay thousands of miles of hostile ocean, deadly sharks, thirst, hunger, enemy aircraft, and eventual incarceration in a Japanese prisoner of war (POW) camp. Driven to the limits of endurance, Zamperini answered desperation with ingenuity. He suffered with hope and faced brutality with rebellion.[4]

Hillenbrand chose Zamperini as the topic for her bestseller for much the same reason she chose Seabiscuit for her previous book: they exemplify exceptional performance in the face of adversity—something that proves impossible if one cannot or will not tolerate ambiguity.

We shouldn't be surprised that Hillenbrand chose to write about how to overcome adversity because she faced the darkness and loneliness of hardship herself. After leading an active childhood, Hillenbrand experienced the sudden onset of a then-unknown sickness at 19. One day while a sophomore at Kenyon College, she suddenly fell violently ill. Three days later, she could hardly sit up and could not walk to class. Terrified and confused, she dropped out of school and returned home.

Hillenbrand's family, friends, and doctors did not understand her illness, and those close to her pulled away, leaving Hillenbrand to battle an unknown disease alone. Eventually, doctors diagnosed her with Chronic Fatigue Syndrome, but not before many had ridiculed her and labeled her lazy. Until late 2015, she rarely left her house because of the condition.

When ambiguity shows up with adversity, they impose themselves without invitation. In these situations, we can link the willingness to *tolerate* ambiguity with the will to overcome adversity to begin a successful next chapter. *Seabiscuit* recounts the story of the transformative power of effort—the power of determination to change situations and outcomes. *Unbroken* and Hillenbrand's biography tell similar stories. Filtered through a stagnant mindset, these represent nice accounts of people playing the cards they were dealt. Looking at them through a lens of disruption, however, we see people deciding to reshuffle the deck, even though they have no way of knowing what the new cards will bring. We see people going beyond tolerating ambiguity to embracing it.

Decisiveness under pressure requires *high-ambiguity tolerance*. When people tolerate, or even appreciate ambiguity, they demonstrate the ability to *synthesize*. As we recall our chemistry classes, synthesis is the production of a substance from simpler materials after a chemical reaction. In life, we must play the role of chemist to create the reaction we want for ourselves and for those who depend on us. Figure 1.2 shows what that looks like.

Decisive leaders, who have little tolerance for ambiguity, can *aggregate* data. That is, they can make decisions based on loosely associated fragments of information. This works under *ordinary* circumstances, but during times of change, especially unexpected, unwelcome change, you'll find little that's ordinary.

The *analyst* doesn't fare so well amid disorder. Their tendency toward indecision, coupled with their intolerance of ambiguity, often explains why

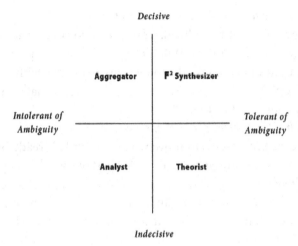

FIGURE 1.2
Ambiguity Tolerance.

a deal fails or ill-advised choices create more problems. Speed of decision-making becomes more important in high-stakes, crisis situations.

Theorists, those who enjoy an element of ambiguity but who find decision-making daunting, won't do much better. Given enough time, they can make the right call, but once again, opportunities appear and disappear quickly.

In *Landing in the Executive Chair*, I first introduced the F^2 *Leader*— leaders who balance fairness and firmness, modeling effective leadership during most situations. However, not all F^2 Leaders have what it takes to make the tough calls when the future seems so ambiguous. During my more than 40 years of studying leadership, I have found leaders make what I call *The Five Typical Wrong Turns* that usually explain why they didn't welcome ambiguity and change:

1. *A focus on process over results*
   Too often leaders become ego-involved with their tactics, defending them, even when a mountain of data suggests they don't work anymore. Usually, this kind of wrong-minded focus causes a temporary setback. In a time of crisis, however, this stagnant mindset can cause dire consequences. Frequently I have worked with clients who refused to admit they were causing their own competition—forcing disruptive thinking to battle with that's-the-way-we've-always-done-things thinking.

2. *A preference for popularity over respect*
Most people want to be liked. But leaders don't get paid to be liked. They get paid for results. When they don't hold people accountable, or when they fail to make the tough calls associated with change, they give people reason not to respect them, which usually makes these same people not like them.

3. *A penchant for perfection, not success*
I encourage my clients to move when they're 80% ready because the time and money required for reaching 100% won't compensate for any added benefits. Of course, some things require accuracy and precision. One side of a door jamb can't differ from the other side by even a fraction of an inch. But those in the C-suite left *those* kinds of decisions to others years prior to their promotions. Those who won't accept imperfection doom themselves and others to the perils of stagnation.

4. *Choosing quick fixes over goal accomplishment*
As much as I champion speed in decision-making, I don't advocate settling for the wrong decision. Too often, in a crisis, leaders want to reduce pain for themselves and others in their companies, so they opt for the quick fix. This action may look decisive and courageous but, without good judgment, it becomes reckless. Honing good judgment involves keeping the long-term consequences for every major decision in view. Leaders who do this eventually enjoy more success.

5. *Seeking harmony at the expense of problem-solving*
People who overvalue popularity frequently also gloss over conflict. They shy away from debate, even though forcing themselves to argue about the crucial components of the deal so often leads to better decisions. When leaders make good hiring decisions and then fail to listen to those smart people, disagree with them, and encourage them to differ with each other, they metaphorically leave smarts on the table—along with the money better decisions would have generated. Effective leaders not only encourage problem-solving; they *invite* others to take an opposing view when facing a high-stakes call.

Each of these wrong turns involves a decision or a series of decisions that takes the leader and others in the organization down the wrong paths. These paths won't always be roads to perdition, but leaders who stay on them too often or too much find they have ended up where they never intended to go. That can't happen too many times before people start to question the talent of those making the decisions and avoid considering them for advancement. Becoming more self-aware, however, can offset dangers.

HOW SELF-AWARENESS AFFECTS MINDSET

Research shows that self-awareness—knowing who we are *and* how others see us—forms the foundation of high performance, smart choices, and lasting relationships. However, people don't see themselves quite as clearly as they could. If they have always had a stagnant mindset, they are loathe to explore the disruption that truly knowing themselves might bring.

Every executive I've ever coached has eventually asked in some form, "Should I *confront* my shortcomings, or should I create a world where I have none?" People don't usually hire me until and unless they are ready to ask this question. The most successful ones never stop asking—thereby creating constant disruption in their lives—disruptions that challenge them and position them for success.

For years, when I gave clients feedback about the data I had gathered, I began on what I considered was a positive note, explaining all the strengths I had uncovered and exploring options for leveraging them in the future. It took several years for me to realize this approach didn't work.

The clients would dutifully feign interest but never ask follow-up questions. Of course, I should have worked this out much sooner than I did because, when I began the session with "What are *your* goals for this session?" invariably, they would answer, "I want to know my weaknesses so I can mitigate them."

I then developed a new technique for presenting the findings. I would tell them that I would give them feedback in four major areas: their decision-making and problem-solving abilities, their approach to work, their approach to people, and their leadership style. I would follow-up with the pluses and minuses in each area—telling them how others perceived them, frequently revealing impressions that clashed with the ways they saw themselves.

Like my best clients, many great leaders confront their shortcomings on a regular basis. Darwin Smith, looking back on his extraordinary performance at Kimberly-Clark, declared, "I never stopped trying to be qualified for the job." Those *not* like Smith surround themselves with worshipers, exile their critics, and quickly lose touch with both reality and self-awareness. Just as often, leaders demonstrate a stagnant mindset at some points in their careers but not others. Lee Iacocca offers an interesting example of this phenomenon.

Iacocca joined the Ford Motor Company in 1946. After a brief stint in engineering, he asked to be moved to sales and marketing, where his career flourished. He gained national recognition for his disruptive approach with his "56 for '56" campaign, offering loans on 1956 model cars with a 20% downpayment and $56 in monthly payments for three years.

In the 1970s, Henry Ford II was the chairman of Ford; Lee Iacocca headed Ford U.S. and Hal Sperlich served as Iacocca's deputy of product design. In 1976, recognizing the American car buyer's need to respond to gas shortages, and certain that the American market would demand smaller cars, Sperlich recommended Ford downsize its automobiles, advocating smaller, more fuel-efficient cars to compete with foreign imports. Even though the Mustang had enjoyed great success in the 1960s, Henry Ford disagreed. He pontificated from the outset that he did not want a small, new, front-wheel-drive car because he didn't think the market would change too much. He advocated taking an existing middle-level Ford car, stripping it down, and making it lighter. That car became known in the dustup as the "Panther," Ford's favorite. It also served as a metaphor for Ford's stagnant mindset.

Even before this debate, in late 1975, after hearing the arguments about how costly a new small-car line would be, Iacocca offered what he considered an inspired idea: Use a Honda engine. Honda's engineering and front-wheel-drive technology had impressed Iacocca, so, after a surreptitious trip to Japan to discuss a joint venture, Iacocca presented his idea to Ford: Build the Fiesta within 18 months with a Honda engine and transmission in it.

Ford reacted with indignation, "No Jap engine is going under the hood of a car with my name on it," he announced. "Small cars mean small profits" became his mantra.

Iacocca and Sperlich agreed with each other about what they wanted the mission to be—respond to customer demands—but Ford disagreed. He wanted to stick with the status quo. The stalemate led to dire consequences. Ford fired Sperlich, and the American car buyer punished Ford Motor

Company.[5] Eventually, Iacocca became the president of the Ford Motor Company, but he clashed with Henry Ford who fired him in 1978, even though the company posted a $2 billion profit for the year.

Iacocca went to Chrysler in 1978 where he served as president and CEO, making him the only executive to preside over the operations of two of the Big Three automakers. The Disruptive Mindset he displayed at Ford did not follow Iacocca to Chrysler, however.

After his initial success, Iacocca kept bringing out the same car models over and over with only superficial changes. Unfortunately, no one wanted these models. Meanwhile, Chrysler's Japanese competitors started giving U.S. customers what they wanted, revamping how cars looked, changing how they ran, and improving how they used gas.

The Iacocca magic, like Chrysler's earnings, faded as the nation dipped into recession. Iacocca started vilifying the Japanese as alien invaders. He argued that Chrysler made better cars, that Japan's "Teflon Kimono" had deceived Americans, and that the U.S. was suffering from a national inferiority complex. His barnstorming backfired. Critics accused him of "Japan bashing" and said Chrysler's rebates suggested a fire sale. Finally surrendering to pressures to step down, Iacocca retired as Chrysler's chairman and chief executive in 1992.

What happened to this man who had once demonstrated the strongest of Disruptive Mindsets? In short, he stagnated. He got comfortable and complacent—the two enemies of disruption. He created a world where he felt secure and content, so he quit learning, changing, innovating, and growing. A stagnant world lures us into thinking that contentment and comfort are good enough.

But was he happy? After coaching hundreds of high-achieving executives for thousands of hours, I have realized an immutable truth: Those who are destined to achieve must achieve, or they won't be happy. That means, if they choose to rest on their laurels, they won't hear lauding from within or without.

CONCLUSION

Why do some organizations embrace change while others fail to do so? Why do some companies make disruption their goal with no clear objective for doing so? A goal to grow a company will inevitably lead to disruption, but a goal to disrupt won't lead to growth. In fact, a goal to change for the sake of change will more likely lead not only to loss of market share, but also loss of both customer loyalty and top performers.

A Disruptive Mindset starts with a clear vision of what should change and what should stay the same. Any other approach will upset the ecosystem of the organization unnecessarily, unreasonably, and unwisely. How we think about our talents and abilities determines our success in every arena of human endeavor and separates the winners from the also-rans or the never-tried.

NOTES

1 Dweck, C. (2001). *Mindset: The New Psychology of Success.* New York: Random House. P. 7.
2 Cutter, C. (2019). "The Best-Managed Companies of 2019." *The Wall Street Journal.* November 25. P. R1.
3 Hillenbrand, L. (2001). *Seabiscuit: An American Legend.* New York: Ballantine Books.
4 Hillenbrand, L. (2010). *Unbroken: A World War II Story of Survival, Resilience, and Redemption.* New York: Random House.
5 Halberstam, D. (1986). *The Reckoning.* New York: William Morrow and Company.

2

Create Disruption or Someone Else Will

The Berlin Wall came down in 1989, but apparently someone forgot to notify the Ahornia deer of the region. They still refuse to cross the line. At the height of the Cold War, an electric fence, barbed wire, and machine-gun-carrying guards cut off Eastern Europe from the Western world, which also severed the herds of deer. All barriers have disappeared, but the red deer haven't changed their behavior. Even though they weren't alive when the border existed or came down, they inherited a predisposition to avoid crossing it.

Apparently, taking a page from the deer handbook, many leaders behave the same way. They don't really know why the silos and processes exist, but their instincts keep them from taking full advantage of the opportunities that would exist if they were not so committed to them. This adherence to the past and fear of disruption has myriad problems, not the least of which involves short-changing strategy formulation and succession planning. Similarly, many of the obligations and constraints we self-impose live on for outdated reasons—and some weren't necessary in the first place. However, when we understand disruption and the people who intentionally create it, we understand how to design it instead of fearing it.

ISN'T DISRUPTION BAD?

I have often said, only partly facetiously, that a leader's second-worst nightmare is an idiot with initiative (their first is a smart narcissist). A Disruptive Mindset definitely requires initiative, but only really smart decision makers can discern why and when they should take a risk.

In previous writing, I have called these exceptional decision makers "virtuoso." They know what it takes to upset the status quo and shift power in relationships. These exceptional thinkers understand why innovation feels easy compared to disruption: primarily because leaders must invite risk to move from the wings to center stage. They recognize that disruption doesn't have to be fast and furious and realize that when the stakes are highest, they must abandon their comfort zones.

Sears, General Electric (GE), Hewlett Packard, Wells Fargo, and Toys "Я" Us—all once-estimable companies—have now suffered the consequences of refusing to disrupt "the way we've always done things around here" thinking. In the 1980s and earlier, Sears was the largest retailer in the U.S. until Walmart and Kmart surpassed it in sales in 1990.

Sears began to diversify, which they needed to do, but these actions distracted senior leaders' attention from the competition. In fact, these decision makers dismissed Walmart's threat because Walmart had lower quality products and few salespeople dedicated to appliances. They also overlooked the fact that appliances turn over slowly and don't significantly contribute to net profit.

As it turned out, Walmart disrupted the status quo by resetting prices for the entire country. At about the same time, California sued Sears for a series of pricing scandals that revealed the company had falsely charged customers for unneeded repairs when they brought their cars in for other reasons. By 2018, Sears, the 31st-largest retailer in the U.S., had filed for Chapter 11 bankruptcy. Sears apparently saw disruption as negative while Walmart embraced it.

In 1981, Jack Welch welcomed disruption too. He became GE's youngest chairman and CEO—and a leader who understood that if he didn't create disruption, someone else would. A year after taking the reins, he had dismantled much of the existing management approaches with aggressive simplification and consolidation. His famous primary leadership directives became to "Make GE No. 1 or No. 2" in the industries in which it participated.

Throughout the 1980s Welch sought to streamline—not necessarily to disrupt—GE, yet under his leadership, GE increased market value from $12 billion in 1981 to $410 billion 21 years later. At the time of his retirement, he had made 600 acquisitions while shifting into emerging markets, thereby recasting the company in a significantly new mold. Welch also worked to eradicate inefficiency by trimming inventories and dismantling the bureaucracy that had almost led him to leave GE earlier in his career. He closed factories, reduced payrolls, and cut lackluster units.

Jeff Immelt, Welch's replacement, took a different governance path, differentiating himself from Welch in both substance and style. On the one hand, Immelt caused some positive disruption with changes in plastics, appliances, workplace diversity, and GE Capital businesses. On the other hand, Immelt found himself immersed in several public controversies. Lassitude, indecision, relaxation of Welch's ethical standards, and the fall of GE stock price by 45% followed Welch's retirement.

Immelt didn't want to inherit the "house that Jack built," so his decisions invited criticism from dividend-oriented investors and board members— when they became aware of decisions, like the one to have an empty corporate jet follow his plane *just in case* there were delays with his primary jet. Immelt created disruption for his own gain, all the while claiming that things were fine.

Without constant innovation and sustainable excellence in senior management and board directors, even the best leaders flounder and founder. That's what happened when Carly Fiorina took the helm at Hewlett-Packard in 1999. Fiorina, whom *Fortune* named the most powerful woman in business in 1998, lost her job at Hewlett-Packard just six years later. Why? She didn't know what to disrupt and what to leave alone, bringing into question her critical thinking abilities.

The company's controversial deal to buy Compaq in the spring of 2002— after a bruising proxy fight led by one of the Hewlett family heirs—did not produce the shareholder returns or profits she had promised. Fiorina either failed to anticipate the implications of and obstacles to her decision to buy Compaq, or she simply didn't pursue feedback that may have revealed errors in her judgment or resistance to her plan. Had she explored multiple perspectives, particularly those of the Hewlett family, she may have been able to identify probable consequences and to avert the temporary plummet in HP stock, widespread job losses, and her own downfall. Both HP and Fiorina paid for her weak leadership intelligence and inability to disrupt effectively.

Wells Fargo has also experienced both positive and negative disruptions. In 1981, Wells Fargo's assistant operations officer, Lloyd Benjamin, perpetrated one of the largest embezzlements in history by successfully writing off phony debit and credit receipts to benefit boxing promoters Muhammed Ali Professional Sports, Inc.

In 2009, the Illinois Attorney General filed suit against Wells Fargo, alleging the bank steered African American and Hispanic customers into high-cost subprime loans that eventually led to a large percentage of foreclosures in minority neighborhoods. In 2010, Wells Fargo acknowledged that between 2004 and 2007 one of its acquired companies, Wachovia, had failed to monitor and report suspected money laundering by narcotics traffickers.

In 2010, a U.S. District Court judge fined Wells Fargo for overdraft practices designed to "gouge" consumers and for misleading consumers about how the bank processed transactions and assessed overdraft fees. In 2012, the government sued Wells Fargo for "reckless" lending. Despite all the drama, Wells Fargo stock closed at its historical high of $65.93 on January 26, 2018. One could argue that decision makers at the company *finally* realized how to leverage disruption.

The lessons either came too late or didn't come at all for Toys "Я" Us. In 1948, Charles Lazarus founded Toys "Я" Us, but by 2017, leaders of the chain had filed for Chapter 11 bankruptcy in response to its $5 billion in long-term debt. At its peak, consumers considered Toys "Я" Us a classic example of a "category killer," a retailer that carries an assortment of products of a given type. Through pricing and market penetrations, these stores create a competitive advantage. We consider Barnes & Noble, Best Buy, and Staples successful category killers. With the rise of mass merchants and online retailers, Toys "Я" Us began to lose its share of the toy market.

Scandals (Sears), succession planning (GE), CEO selection (HP), a flawed value system (Wells Fargo), and greed (Toys "Я" Us) played roles in the collapse of companies we once appreciated. Is this the inescapable future for companies that fail to disrupt in the right ways?

Disruption means bridging the gap between what's happening and what's possible. It can come by invitation, or it can show up like a drunk wedding crasher. Good or bad? More depends on the *response* to the commotion than on the disruption itself. Leaders who want to grow and innovate need to understand their own reactions to disruption and to have the tools for creating a safe environment for experimentation for those in the trenches. To answer the question: "Isn't disruption bad?" the answer seems clear: It will be if it doesn't lead to growth.

DISRUPTIVE GROWTH

In *Landing in the Executive Chair*, I described "A players" and "high potentials" as *virtuosos*. Virtuosos distinguish themselves by exemplifying what I call the E^5 Star Performer Model: Excellence, Expertise, Experience, Enterprise, and Ethics. They force people to take them seriously. They don't raise the bar—they set it for everyone else. They serve as gold standards for what people should strive to be and attain. If you were to scour the world, you'd be hard-pressed to find people who do their jobs better. You wouldn't hesitate to hire them again, and you'd be crushed if you found out they were leaving.

Others look to virtuosos for guidance and example. Often they consider virtuosos edgy and contrarian, but they seldom ignore them. Virtuosos chafe at too much supervision or tight controls—fortunately, they need neither. They constantly search for the new horizon and welcome the unforeseen challenge. No synonym for the word "virtuoso" exists. Some might substitute "artist," "expert," or "musician," but these don't suffice. Many can lay claim to these titles and still fail to be virtuosos. Few virtuosos exist. These hardy individuals go beyond resilience to grow—even after confronting adversity.

The general understanding that disruption often yields positive change is not a new one. Some of the early ideas and writing of the ancient Hebrews and Greeks, and religious teaching of Christianity, Hinduism, Buddhism, and Islam contain elements of the potentially transformative power of disruptions, usually described as suffering. Attempts to understand and discover the meaning of human travails represent a central theme of much philosophical inquiry and appear in the works of novelists, dramatists, and poets. Not until the mid-1990s, however, did psychologists Richard Tedeschi and Lawrence Calhoun coin the term *Post-Traumatic Growth* (PTG).

According to these theorists, PTG explains the transformation that follows trauma and holds that people who endure psychological struggle following adversity can often see growth afterward. Many consider PTG synonymous with resilience. They contend that becoming more resilient as a result of struggle can be an example of PTG, but Tedeschi and others of his ilk disagree.

As they posit, someone who is *already* resilient when trauma occurs won't experience PTG. These theorists argue that because resilient people don't feel *rocked to their core* by an event, they don't have to seek a new belief system as a result of it. *Less* resilient people, they contend, often go through distress and confusion as they try to understand why this terrible thing happened to them. Their struggle to find resilience *causes* their growth.

I don't concur. My research on war veterans causes me to conclude that the more resilient the person *before* the trauma or disruption, the better the chances of growing afterward. Even though Tedeschi and Calhoun don't agree with me about the state of the person *facing* the disruption, we do agree about how growth can happen after it. They posit that PTG occurs in five general areas: appreciation of life, relationships with others, new possibilities in life, personal strength, and spiritual change.

According to them, these five factors determine an individual's progress in reconstructing their perceptions of self, others, and the meaning of events while they are coping with the aftermath of trauma. My research mirrors these conclusions and offers the following ten benefits to disruption virtuosos can enjoy:

1. *Personal growth*

   A disruption often causes a shift in power, and people discover what they're made of. They discover they are stronger than they ever realized. They learn optimism, deepen their spirituality, and develop the confidence to say, "I now know that I can better handle difficulties because I have." They set priorities in their lives and gain a feeling of self-mastery and learn they can control more than they ever imagined.

2. *A focus on vision, not tactics*

   In addition to setting new priorities for themselves, those who have slain the dragon of adversity learn to reevaluate threats and opportunities, rationally evaluating the risks *and* the rewards. They start asking, "If we weren't already doing this, would we decide to start now?" They position themselves for success, focusing on decisions that will improve their condition, not merely on problem-solving that will return things to the status quo. They don't settle for *surviving* which is reaching the *previous* level of functioning before a trauma, stressor, or disruption. They insist on *thriving*, which goes above and beyond resilience and involves finding benefits within the disruption.

3. *A willingness to kill sacred cows*

   Although the term "future-proofing" came into the vernacular in 2007 in relation to sustainable design, COVID-19 caused the term to become a catchphrase for all that must happen to anticipate the future and develop methods of minimizing the effects of the shock of things that haven't yet happened. Those who choose to kill sacred cows and future-proof will design something that will be useful and successful *when*, not *if*, the situation changes.

By abandoning conventional mindsets and questioning long-held assumptions about revenue streams, customers, culture, and operations, virtuosos take performance to a new level for themselves, their teams, and their organization.

4. *Formation of a culture of innovation, not caution*
Ordinarily, culture should serve as a strong stabilizing force; however, the root of culture is "cult," a testament to the kind of thinking that can often guide decision makers to adhere to a mindset that no longer works. But just as leaders can encourage cult-like thinking, they can stimulate a culture of growth. A change in operating practices or strategy does not constitute a desertion of all that is "holy," but only those organizations that create a true culture of innovation can help their people understand the difference. An agile, flexible, and fast-paced organization thrives on the edge of disruption.

5. *Speed*
Pre-pandemic, we took for granted that implementing anything new would take a long time—or at least as long as it had always taken. As doctors scrambled to discover vaccines, tests, and treatments for COVID-19, they realized they could move faster than they ever had and certainly faster than they'd ever been forced to. This sort of mindset shift caused many to believe Oliver Wendell Holmes when he said, "A mind that is stretched by a new experience can never go back to its old dimensions" or Nathan Bradford Forrest when he was erroneously quoted as saying, "Git thar fustest with the most mostest."

6. *Agility and efficiency, the complexity cures*
William of Occam, an English Franciscan friar and scholastic philosopher, has influenced modern organizational theory—but not enough. *Occam's Razor*—the shaving away of all that is unnecessary—suggests parsimony, economy, and succinctness in problem-solving. It states that the fewest assumptions should be selected—the fewer the better—even though more complicated conclusions might also prove correct.

New strategies that fail to significantly improve efficiency will have little chance of success. Companies will feel the pressure to provide value for money and to streamline operations, which may bring parts of the supply chain closer to home and away from lower-cost countries.

For each accepted explanation of a phenomenon, an infinite number of possible and more complex alternatives exists. But these alternatives cost more in time and resources—and they impede growth. As Occam noted, "It is vain to do with more what can be done with less." Vain perhaps. Bad business—definitely.

7. *Improved personal and professional relationships*
During the self-isolation period of COVID-19, one of my best clients reported that he instituted a virtual Zoom "hall meeting" every week for direct reports to share non-work stories about their families and hobbies. This one small act caused at least one team to greatly improve its cohesion because people simply learned more about each other. A dog barking, a cat jumping in front of the screen, or a little one toddling into the meeting didn't distract. These small slices of life created new focus on the relationships people had taken for granted—often for years.

8. *New customers*
Negative disruption, like a global pandemic, creates new customer problems that demand quick solutions. Restaurant owners who emerged successfully from lockdown orders in 2020 almost immediately started offering curbside pick-up, family meal deals, and carry-out menus they had never considered before. Many owners reported they acquired new customers who had never patronized their restaurants previously. These owners learned it was never about technology or competition. Growth had *always* been about finding new customers who had become unhappy with their other options.

9. *A more flexible labor pool and hiring practices*
Companies that were once dead set against remote work began to see tangible advantages in the "work from home" orders. Most people didn't have to be in the office to do their jobs. In fact, for some of my clients, people became *more* productive because of less time commuting, less burnout, and better work/life balance.

As companies emerged from the crisis, they realized they could source talent globally since technology allows companies to search the planet to find the *best* person for the job, not just the one who lives in the same geographical location. Also, employees of the future are likely to choose small towns and rural communities when they don't have to add an hour's commute each way to their days, leading to economic growth in areas hard-hit after the recession of 2008.

10. *More telemedicine, leading to a reduction in health costs*
When clinics and doctors' offices closed during the COVID-19 pandemic, patients and healthcare providers stumbled upon ideas for improving care and reducing costs. They found that patients were more likely to seek health care when they could do it from the convenience of their homes. This improved general wellness because people didn't wait until they were sick to seek a doctor's help. Visits were cheaper, and for the first time, people in rural areas had more choices in quality health care.

Growth after disruption, whether traumatic or less daunting, can happen, but it won't happen automatically. Much will depend on decision makers learning lessons quickly and adapting adeptly. Sometimes these virtuosos will emerge *because* of the crisis, but just as often, they will be the exceptional people leaders always depended on to accelerate growth. They won't always fall into the category of the well-behaved, however.

WELL-BEHAVED PEOPLE SELDOM MAKE HISTORY

British author Mary Anne Evans, who used the pen name George Eliot, once advised, "The important work of moving the world forward does not wait to be done by perfect men." The same can be said of virtuosos who create disruption that leads to recovery after a crisis. These flawed but bold individuals have always played a role in major change, and they will continue to do so into the future.

Greta Thunberg is one such person. Born in Sweden in 2003, this young environmental activist gained international recognition for promoting the view that humanity faces a crisis arising from climate change. Known for her youth and straightforward speaking, she criticized world leaders for their failure to take enough action to address the climate crisis.

By the age of 15, she had started spending her school days outside the Swedish Parliament protesting their decisions. Soon other students joined her. Her efforts led her to address the United Nations Climate Action Summit in 2019 with accusations of "How dare you?" The press and others took up the clarion cry that came to be called "The Greta Effect." *Time Magazine* named her to the 100 Most Influential People List and the youngest Person of the Year. *Forbes* listed her as one of The World's 100 Most Powerful Women in 2019, and she received two consecutive nominations for the Nobel Peace Prize in 2019 and 2020. She may have been the youngest person to be mentioned in these esteemed publications, but she wasn't the best behaved.

Neither was Arianna Huffington. A Republican turned Democrat and a critic of early feministic writing turned feminist author, Huffington served as a vanguard to show us the future of online communications. She demonstrated ways to personalize media, share content on a new platform, and totally democratize the news. She cofounded *The Huffington Post*, started Thrive Global, and authored 15 books. *Time* and *Forbes* also singled her out for recognition. At times perspicacious, often humorous, Huffington challenged the mundane and claimed to have spent hours fending off inquisition from her nasty "inner-dialogue roommate" who pointed out her every flaw. People have described her as "impish," "wickedly funny," and "wacky." I choose to call her "disruptive."

Also disrupting social mores and customs, Ayaan Hirsi Ali burst into international headlines following the murder of Theo van Gogh by an Islamist who threatened that Ali would be next. She made headlines again when the Dutch government threatened to strip her of her citizenship and forced her to resign from the Dutch Parliament.

Her high public profile and outspokenness continued to attract controversy after she emigrated to the U.S. In 2007, the local Muslim community protested Ali's planned lecture at the University of Pittsburgh, with one activist claiming she deserved the death sentence, not a place of honor at a university.

Raised in a strict Muslim family, Hirsi Ali survived civil war, female mutilation, and brutal beatings. Reactionary Islamists demonized her; her family disowned her, and others threatened her, yet she refused to be silenced. As a distinguished political superstar and champion of free speech, her iron will and extraordinary determination to fight injustice allowed her to triumph over adversity to emerge an outspoken pioneer of freedom—not well behaved, but certainly disruptive.

A headmaster once told British business magnate Richard Branson, who has an estimated net worth of $4.4 billion, that he would either end up in prison or become a millionaire. He chose the latter. American entrepreneur Mark Cuban, who worked as a bartender and was fired from his job as a salesperson for Your Business Software, now has an estimated worth of $4.3 billion.

Renowned inventor Thomas Edison set off a media sensation in 1920 when he told a reporter that he was working on a spirit phone that would allow communication with the dead. He later admitted it had all been a joke.

Robin Olds, a U.S. Air Force fighter pilot and triple ace shot down a total of 17 enemy aircraft during World War II and the Vietnam War. Military historians regard him as the best wing commander of the Vietnam War, both for his air-fighting skills and his reputation as a combat leader.

Historians also remember him for his extravagantly waxed and decidedly non-regulation mustache. It was a common superstition among aviators that growing a "bulletproof mustache" would protect them in combat. But Olds went a step further. He used his mustache as a sign of defiance, pointing out that "It became the middle finger I couldn't raise in the PR photographs." He used this gesture again in 1967 shortly after he took command of the U.S. Air Force Academy.

After his return from Vietnam, the newly promoted General Olds reported to the Chief of Staff of the Air Force, General John P. McConnell, who pointed to the now famous mustache and ordered, "Take it off." Olds complied, ending the era of the bulletproof mustache. But the cadets at the academy had ideas about extending the tenure of the facial hair. As Olds took the stage to be introduced, 3,000+ cadets greeted him with black paper mustaches they donned in unison. In a light-hearted response, Olds displayed the aforementioned middle finger to the Cadet Wing while hiding it from the Cadet Staff and officers seated on the elevated seating area behind him, once again proving that those who don't disrupt seldom make history.

What do these examples have in common? Not everyone with a Disruptive Mindset makes it on to the lists of *Time* and *Forbes*, but they do share other characteristics. They show a willingness to question what they've always believed, leverage their smarts, set demanding goals, self-regulate, and emerge from the changed reality ready to tackle challenges. Philosopher John Dewey observed, "Saints engage in introspection while burly sinners run the world." These burly sinners will help themselves and everyone else emerge from crisis, but they will also innovate in whatever reality comes. They are the virtuosos among us.

WHICH COMES FIRST, BEHAVIOR OR MINDSET?

Generating explanations for human behavior has been a pastime since humans started having pastimes. Theoretical systems evolve as people try to account for individual differences in behavior and beliefs. Why do people behave the way they do? Why do behavioral differences exist? How do our beliefs drive our behavior and vice versa? Attempts to answer these questions have kept social and behavioral scientists busy, but clearly no definitive conclusions have been forthcoming. Each theorist offers alternative perspectives for examining similarities and differences and for explaining how both our mindsets and behaviors develop.

Even though expounding on possible reasons for human behavior has occurred for centuries, psychology is a new science. Psychology, which emerged as an independent scientific discipline in Germany during the middle of the nineteenth century, defined its task as the analysis of consciousness in the normal, adult human being. Psychologists became single-minded in their quest to discover the basic elements of consciousness that determine how these elements form our "mental chemistry."

Different camps began to argue that the main function of the mind, or consciousness, has to do with its *active* processes rather than with its *passive* contents. Sensing, not sensations; thinking, not ideas; imagining, not images—these *actions* should be the principal subject of psychology, these theorists contended. Others argued that the private, subjective mind does not lend itself to investigation; only *observable* behaviors would hold the answers.

Erik Erikson, a German psychoanalytic psychologist, built on earlier work by giving special attention to the role of *ego* in human development and its role in growth and positive functioning. Erikson postulated that human development occurs in eight predetermined stages that lead us to develop an *identity*. According to Erikson, identity consists of the things within people, what they become, and what they are supposed to become. Therefore, a person's vocation, the support society gives the individual for this choice, and the internalization of the ideals of the environment determine identity.

According to Erikson, trust or mistrust develops during infancy, from birth to one year. During this first year of life, the child whose needs are met both emotionally and physically begins to sense that the world is a safe place. In contrast, a child whose needs are ignored, whose world is chaotic and unpredictable, begins to fear the world and becomes suspicious of it.

Literature about the Holocaust implies that trauma can interfere with the continued development of hardiness—and the younger the person is at the time of the trauma, the more dramatic the interference. While most prisoners of the Holocaust suffered greatly, the traumatic effects were intensified in individuals who were children at the time of their incarceration. As we learned, trauma reduces the ability to cope and adjust in everyone, but it disproportionately troubles the young. Most shocking ordeals not only *retroactively* affect the past by causing us not to remember them, they also cause us to remember only negative memories from that time. Similarly, problems can also *proactively* contaminate all subsequent events.

Nearly everyone agrees that trauma to children has dire effects, but not everyone agrees about how we acquire our talents for coping with disaster. In fact, theorists have been waging the "nature/nurture" battle for centuries. Plato, Aristotle, Machiavelli, and Hippocrates were some of the early "nature" theorists. These names don't often appear in psychology texts, but each had something to say about the "Which came first?" question.

Each philosopher attempted to do justice to the complexity and uniqueness of the individual, some emphasizing the importance of conscious motives, some focused on the past, others convinced we are creatures of the present. Like all theories, each has its critics. Some give too much attention to what goes on inside the person and not enough credit to the impact of the environment. Others do the opposite.

Another school of thought concentrated primarily on the scientific understanding of the *learning* process. Assuming people learn most behavior, they contended, we concentrate on acquiring a multitude of behaviors that allow us to survive and prosper in transactions with the environment—constantly seeking pleasure and avoiding pain.

No universally embraced theory exists. The nature/nurture debate continues with added and complex elements surfacing with each new theory, and no one has arbitrated the dispute about whether the past or present has a more profound effect on behavior. Further, investigators disagree about the uniqueness of the individual versus the uniformity of the species. Some theorists drastically conflict, and others build on each other.

Behavior and mindset both give glimpses into a person's personality, but they do more. They also demonstrate how a person deals with emotionally significant things. Interpersonal relationships, especially our early ones, play a role too. We learn behaviors from our parents that eventually shape our beliefs.

For instance, many parents start taking their babies to church services far before the children understand dogma. In addition to hearing the revered text and singing the sacred songs, these children participate in rituals, attend community events, and build relationships with other church members. Drawing from this example, we might infer that behavior comes first.

However, none of this is unidirectional. Just as we constantly send and receive messages to and from the environment, we continuously send and receive *internal* messages that shape our beliefs and behaviors.

On the one hand, we can choose behaviors based on our beliefs—a head first, behavior later bias. Most change-management consultants lead with this approach. They try to uncover the basic beliefs that drive behaviors and to influence or change these beliefs. In fact, much of the work on organizational culture has its genesis in this approach.

That's not how others tackle it, however. The Social Actions programs in the Air Force, to which I referred in Chapter 1, serve as a prime example. As we developed large-scale training programs, at no time did anyone address core beliefs. On the contrary, the message from above seemed loud and clear, "Believe whatever you like, but this is how we expect you to *behave.*" Behavior modification programs in schools operate in much the same way. Teachers tell students what they expect them to do and then reward or punish them accordingly. Teachers in religious schools delve deeper, but even they constantly deal with the *obvious* behaviors, not the beliefs that drive them.

Sometimes we defend behaviors because of our beliefs, and sometimes we rationalize beliefs because of our behaviors. We live in a constant state of flux, seeking always to reduce cognitive dissonance—that annoying state of having *inconsistent* thoughts, beliefs, or attitudes, especially related to behavioral decisions and attitude change.

Just as often, we profess to believe something to justify our behavior. For example, I may say that I always buy Maytag appliances because I think they are the best. However, when pressed for evidence, I may admit that I buy Maytag because my mother always did, and I've been too lazy to find out whether any data actually support this conclusion. We see this kind of "behavior first" phenomenon in families that vote for the same political candidates, pursue careers in the same vein, eat the same kinds of food, buy the same cars, and celebrate life's events similarly.

We also see it frequently in organizations that require new employees to fit into the established culture. People may firmly believe that bribing in foreign countries is immoral but engage in this activity nonetheless if their bosses require them to do so. Other people may harbor strong biases against a certain group but behave as though they don't because they know discriminatory actions would land them in the unemployment lines.

When people behave in ways that contradict their beliefs, one of two things happens: either they leave the environment that created the cognitive dissonance, or they adjust their attitudes to keep their belief system more in line with the behaviors others expect of them. Sometimes this means they become more open to different perspectives, often based on new knowledge. At other times, they have a true conversion.

The chicken-or-egg question about what comes first leads to interesting psychological discourse but few definitive answers. Which comes first? Doesn't really matter. By the time people show up to work, they will adhere to certain beliefs and behave in predictable ways—usually. The role of the leader is to identify those whose mindset and behaviors indicate a willingness and ability to cause the disruption to the status quo that will ultimately lead to an improved condition. You don't have a Disruptive Mindset? *Behave* as if you do until you do.

DISRUPTING SILOS MAKES SENSE

As my clients emerged from the global economic turmoil that began in 2008, they indicated they had learned numerous lessons—the most important one: When leaders make good decisions, little else matters. When they refuse to make decisions, or show a pattern of making bad decisions, *nothing* else matters. As I helped these leaders position themselves for the new economy, I began to see what others didn't see. Something was standing in their way—usually the unwillingness or inability to demand cohesion and teamwork. In many cases, they thought they needed more— more education, more experience, more time, or more data. They didn't realize they had enough of *these*, but they did lack the confidence, courage, and optimism to disrupt.

Through our work together, the most successful leaders realized they could no longer *push* growth. Instead, they had to remove barriers to success—usually barriers of their own making. They needed to understand how to remove their silo-*building* behaviors and replace them with silo-*busting* decisions.

Research offers overwhelming evidence that groups of extremely bright and talented individuals often appreciably *underperform* when compared to groups comprised of average or above-average talent. Too often leaders think they've done their jobs by collecting the individual virtuosos. Then they retreat to a safe distance to watch the innovative fireworks. Frequently, however, instead of engendering "ooh's and ahh's," the group—which never formed into a team—causes a hugely expensive dud. Even while in the same room, they remain in their silos.

Building a team of exceptional people involves appreciating how individual members' characteristics and personalities unite to form the unique culture of a virtuoso team. Satisfaction, performance, productivity, effectiveness, and turnover depend, to a large degree, on the socio-emotional make-up of the team. But one thing remains constant: Stars commonly think they lose their ability to shine when in a galaxy—their distinctive quality diminishing as others shine beside them. Consistently teams underperform despite all the extra resources—problems with coordination, motivation, and fear of losing control chipping away at the benefits of collaboration.

Leaders who aspire to assemble a team of top performers face daunting obstacles if they don't shape and build the team at the onset. Without structure, a team of stars will flounder unproductively, often concluding that the team's efforts are a waste of time, at which time the team founders. Conversely, when leaders define expectations, impose constraints, and help members clarify norms, roles, and responsibilities, the team can spend its time carrying out the task.

Leaders find themselves most motivated to spend on silo busting when the team faces a roadblock, but often that will be too late. A more proactive approach would be to do the *building* of the team when it's actually forming or when things are going well. When leaders disrupt a collection of egos and insist on collaboration, they create a galaxy of stars—a team of virtuosos (see Figure 2.1).

No two teams, not even two teams of stars, look alike. However, when they understand the universal dynamics that contribute to successful interactions among exceptional people, leaders can adapt and adjust their communication to the situation and make choices that will benefit the team and the organization. It all starts with trust.

The willingness to be vulnerable—to link one's own success to another's— starts with the fundamental belief that members care about each other.

High Performing Team

FIGURE 2.1
The High Performing Team.

They don't necessarily feel protected or nurtured, but they don't fear they will be sacrificed on the corporate altar if things go awry either. Virtuosos repeat an internal mantra: "If I sink or swim as a result of *your* efforts, you'd better be a good swimmer yourself and someone who will throw me a lifeline if I need it." When that caliber and quantity of trust pervade the team's interactions, accountability follows.

Problems surface when members haven't established clear lines of responsibility, don't communicate, and haven't clarified publicly what each person needs to do. Ambiguity reigns and establishes itself as the enemy of accountability, which compromises commitment. This lack of understanding creates barriers among team members that significantly impede efficient and effective teamwork. Successful teams keep the spotlight on the *decisions* the team makes, not just on tasks accomplished.

Conventional approaches to understanding teams usually address the *work* the team performs—the tasks they accomplish by functioning collectively rather than individually. When you create a galaxy of stars, however, the emphasis shifts. You assemble stars when you need bold decisions and stellar analytical reasoning—not all hands on deck.

In *Landing in the Executive Chair*, I used the team aboard Apollo 13 to demonstrate how exceptional people working together can achieve unprecedented success, even during a time of crisis. On April 11, 1970 James Lovell commanded the third Apollo mission that was intended to land on the moon. Apollo 13 launched successfully, but the crew had to abort the moon landing after an oxygen tank ruptured, severely damaging the spacecraft's electrical system. Despite great hardship caused by limited power, loss of cabin heat, shortage of water, illness, and the critical need to reengineer the carbon dioxide removal system, the crew returned safely to Earth on April 17. Even though the crew did not accomplish its mission of landing on the moon, the operation was termed a "successful failure" because the astronauts returned safely. It also remains a case study in exceptional teamwork.

Author and researcher Meredith Belbin began using the term "Apollo Syndrome" for a different reason. After assembling teams of people who had sharp, analytical minds and high mental ability, he discovered that the teams don't always or even usually achieve the success that Lovell and his crew enjoyed. In fact, Belbin discovered that when these kinds of teams developed a "failure is not an option" mentality, often they committed collusion in their own failure. They spent excessive time in abortive or destructive debate, trying to persuade other team members to adopt their own views, demonstrating a flair for spotting weaknesses in others' arguments. In short, they never learned to resolve conflict. Some teams never do.

Improved communication, whether it takes place to resolve a conflict, foster trust, or convey respect is key to construction disruption, but we don't always communicate effectively in the best of times, so what are the chances we will in high-stakes situations? For example, during game six of the 2011 World Series, Cardinal player Matt Holliday made an error that would have embarrassed a high school player—he dropped an easy fly ball to left field. As he and Rafael Furcal collided, the game looked more like a *Three Stooges* episode than a competition involving world-class athletes. Why? Two words: "It's mine." Holliday didn't say them.

The same thing happens in organizations every day. So-called "teams," which really resemble committees, fail to determine areas of accountability among their players. Metaphorically, they too drop the ball because no one steps up, yells "Mine!" and makes things happen. Instead, members of the group plod along, neglect defining roles, overlook common goals, and don't hold themselves and each other accountable. This sort of behavior, typical though it may be, frustrates nearly everyone, but it disproportionately de-motivates top performers who want to play a bigger game—one where people don't drop balls. One player can't go to the World Series any more than one solo performer—no matter how great—can carry the organization, but when people understand their roles, great things can happen.

Members of an athletic team may have personal agendas (I want to score the most baskets; I hope to gain the attention of a scout etc.). But winning teams don't let these goals stand at cross-purposes with the team's objective: win the game. In business, unless the leader articulates a clear direction for the team, there is a real risk that different members will pursue their own agendas.

When tackling a major initiative, effective leaders realize they need to assemble a diverse team of phenomenally successful individuals—and then force them to work together. A team composed of *dissimilar,* highly educated specialists often holds the keys to the success of the challenging initiatives. Paradoxically, the qualities required for success are the same ones that will undermine success. Complicated projects demand different skills, but we tend to trust most those who share the most in common with us. Similarly, complex endeavors require highly skilled participants, but they tend to fight with one another, as we learned from the team that discovered insulin. When success hinges on cohesive efforts, leaders need to uncover ways for specialists to work together, under high pressure, in a "no retake" environment.

Strengthening an organization's capacity for collaboration requires a combination of long-term investments—in building relationships and trust and in developing a culture in which leaders model cooperation. It won't happen automatically, but through careful attention to the eight functions of a virtuoso team and the eight things that build collaboration, leaders can solve complex business problems without inducing the destructive behaviors that can accompany the collaborative efforts of stars.

Formation of a top-performing team relies on two kinds of leadership: the external leader and the shared leadership that exists among the team members. Think of the external leader as the coach of the athletic team. The coach's most important responsibilities involve selecting the team, training them, and then guiding them during the game. At the start of the game, the team huddles around the coach for final words of motivation, but once the buzzer sounds, the players take the field to perform—dependent on each other but independently of the coach. That's when the shared leadership kicks in. Sometimes the balance doesn't occur, however, and a team relies too heavily on the external coach.

Unlike a sports team, in an organization a team of stars doesn't *work* together as much as it *thinks* together. Traditionally, people have focused on a division of labor in work groups; however, top-performing teams require a shift in paradigms—a movement toward and focus on a division of *knowledge*. The knowledge that each member offers forms the foundation of that person's contribution and reputation. The collective resources, therefore, of the team combine to explain its resourcefulness.

Creating your galaxy begins with a constellation of stars—people whose performance distinguishes them from the ordinary and whose gravitational pull allows the organization to serve as a magnet to other stars in the solar system. It all starts with the individual but quickly becomes more about the stars orbiting one another in a way that builds cohesive, collaborative efforts.

CONCLUSION

Growth demands that successful business leaders understand they must build cohesion among disparate personalities and functions. Only then can they begin to understand disruption and the people who are *willing and able* to cause it and the growth it can engender. When leaders instill an appreciation of disruption in their teams, they, and everyone around them, can *cause* it instead of *fearing* it. Only then can the organization achieve the success that will guarantee the virtuoso stays and performs well.

Disruption often shows up at the party more by imposition than invitation. Sometimes it will kick in the door, as it did when COVID-19 hit; at other times it will ease in, hiding in the shadows, trying not to draw attention to itself. However it arrives, you might as well invite it in. It plans to stay anyway as either an unwelcome intruder or as a valued guest.

3

Disruption Is Mandatory

MBA students learn to use the expected monetary value (EMV) to evaluate risky opportunities. An individual's reaction to risk, however, is far more complex. In fact, individuals seldom consistently fall neatly into the *risk-neutral*, *risk-averse*, or *risk-seeking* categories. We vary in our reactions, depending on the situation and myriad other factors in our lives. Often senior leaders, board members, economists, and analysts treat *risk aversion* as a preference, but at other times, they act as agents for and champions of change.

In trying to identify all the risks a firm faces, decision makers can turn risk management into an overwhelming paper-processing exercise that distracts them from focusing on the decisions that really matter—the strategic ones that define the firm's success or threaten its existence. When they don't grasp the assumptions and limitations of complex and costly Enterprise Risk Management (ERM) tools and models, these decision makers frequently operate under a false sense of security. Some of them might even consider themselves innovative thinkers. However, few companies have been bold enough to introduce genuinely disruptive innovations—the kind that result in the creation of entirely new markets and business models. To do so requires them to improve their abilities to spot risks, evaluate them, and then grow *because* of them not *in spite of them*.

BLACK SWANS, GRAY RHINOS, AND WHITE ELEPHANTS

The phrase "black swan" originated in the second century when most people assumed that black swans didn't exist. They were wrong. Today, we describe unpredictable, rare events as black swans when they don't fit our expectations. Companies now count on their leaders to recognize that black swans exist and to identify them *before* the competition does. Traditional ERM processes, however, don't spot black swans because this approach too often involves an examination of *past* performance—not future opportunities. Success-minded leaders do better. They understand how to *create* disruption, not react to it.

For example, in 1983 Motorola introduced the world's first cell phone. In 1987, Nokia launched *its* first mobile phone. No one paid attention to Apple. By 2018, 95% of Americans owned a cell phone of some kind, and 77% of those were smartphones.

Leaders at Nokia and Motorola probably thought of Apple as a computer company, but shouldn't Apple's application for a patent have mobilized those making mobile phones to suspect a black swan might be lurking? By definition, Black Swans are unforeseeable, risky events—*unknown unknowns*. Individually, these events are highly improbable, but collectively they occur far more frequently than one might expect.

Black Swans share three principal characteristics: unpredictability, massive impact, and less randomness than they once appeared. The 2008 financial crisis serves as a clear example. Lehman Brothers, the fourth-largest investment bank, with a 158-year history, filed for the biggest bankruptcy in U.S. history on September 15, 2008, sending global markets plummeting. Other noteworthy examples include the 9/11 attacks and the dot-com crash. All were unexpected, but their effects only became clear *after* the fact.

In the opinion of risk analyst Nassim Taleb, Black Swans underlie almost everything about our world, from the rise of religions to events in our own personal lives. Why do we not acknowledge the phenomenon of Black Swans until *after* they occur? Because humans are hardwired to learn *specifics* when they should be focused on *generalities*. We concentrate on things we already know, and continually fail to take into consideration what we *don't* know. That renders us unable to estimate opportunities accurately. Too often we give into the impulse to simplify, narrate, and categorize and fail to reward those who can imagine the "impossible."

For years, Taleb studied how we fool ourselves into thinking we know more than we actually do. We restrict our thinking to the irrelevant and inconsequential, while large events continue to surprise us and shape our world in technology, science, business, and culture. According to Taleb, managers make some common mistakes when confronting risk:

1. They try to anticipate *extreme* events. As the world gets more connected, Black Swans are becoming more consequential, yet we still hold onto blind spots, illusions, and biases. We can retrain ourselves to overcome our cognitive biases and to appreciate randomness. But it's not easy.
2. They study the *past* for guidance. Black Swans are highly consequential but unlikely events that are easily explainable—but only in retrospect.
3. They disregard advice about what *not* to do and follow to the letter advice about what *to do*. However, expert advice is often useless and most forecasting pseudoscience.[1]

You can hedge against negative Black Swans while benefiting from positive ones, but that's not easy either. The biggest mistake leaders make? Companies that ignore Black Swans, both positive and negative, will go under. But instead of trying to anticipate Black Swans, decision makers should reduce their companies' overall vulnerability by identifying Black Swans early and preparing through scenario testing, early warning indicators, and contingency plans.

In 2013, Michele Wucker, a policy analyst who specializes in the world economy and crisis anticipation, coined the term *Gray Rhino*. She used it to identify such events as Hurricane Katrina, the collapse of the Minnesota bridge in 2007, cyberattacks, wildfires, lettuce recalls, and the immigration crisis. Gray Rhinos are not random surprises, however. They occur *after* a series of warnings and *visible* evidence. Nevertheless, leaders often ignore them or minimize them until it's too late.

Black Swan refers to highly *improbable* but highly consequential events, while Gray Rhinos exist out in the open for the world to see. Gray Rhinos create *probable*, high-impact yet ignored threats, similar to but not exactly like both the elephant in the room and the improbable and unforeseeable Black Swan.

Leaders do well to think of Gray Rhinos as *known unknowns*. Instead of helplessly ignoring the obvious trends or waiting to see what happens, savvy leaders take the reins to lead the rhino in the direction that makes most sense for the organization.[2]

For instance, the rise of Netflix and the demise of Blockbuster occurred over many years. In 2000, Blockbuster passed up an offer to buy Netflix for $50 million. If they had spotted the Gray Rhino in the guise of Netflix's distribution system, they would have made a different decision and avoided bankruptcy in 2010, but they didn't. Because Netflix was in its infancy and the web still nascent technology, Blockbuster didn't give it high marks as an acquisition target. By the end of 2019, Netflix would be worth more than $100 billion.

Why do decision makers keep ignoring obvious dangers before they spiral out of control? Weak signals don't create the problems; weak *responses* to signals do. To overcome inertia and deal with Gray Rhinos, the company needs to establish organizational processes and incentives to increase agility. Too often, however, disruptive ideas get buried in the flotsam and jetsam of corporate bureaucracy and rigidity, *creating* instead of *solving* the problems associated with dealing with elephantine problems and opportunities.

The term "white elephant" originated with the King of Siam's practice of giving rare albino *elephants* to courtiers who had displeased him. His subjects considered the animals sacred, but laws protected them from labor. Consequently, receiving a white elephant from a monarch was simultaneously a blessing and a curse. It was a blessing because the animal was sacred and a sign of the monarch's favor but also a curse because the recipient now had an expensive-to-maintain animal he could not give away and could not put to much practical use. The upkeep costs alone could cripple the beneficiary. Today, a white elephant also refers to an extravagant but impractical gift that cannot be easily disposed.

Business leaders see *White Elephants* as observable, difficult-to-address risks. Leaders find taking decisive actions hard because these situations trigger fear—fear of failure, rejection, change, or loss of control. These often-unfounded fears cause leaders to consider the wrong kinds of information or to rely too heavily on the status quo. We often cling to the status quo because the comfort of it lies deep within our psyches. In a desire to protect our egos, we resist taking action that may also involve responsibility, blame, and regret, and other emotions nearly everyone wants to avoid.

White Elephants are extant, existential risks that people don't want to address. Fraught with subjectivity, emotions, and loyalties, these no-win situations often prevent decisive actions. A classic "elephant in the room" example is a money-losing initiative favored by the CEO. These situations are *known knowns*—significant problems that leaders understand but feel helpless or at least reluctant to address.[3] To deal with White Elephants, leaders move past indecision and good intentions and focus on decisive solutions to change the status quo.

THE STATUS QUO CAN BE RISKIER THAN CHANGE

We base most important decisions on our beliefs about the likelihood of *uncertain* events, such as the outcome of an election, the guilt of a defendant, or the future success of a stock. We typically express these beliefs with statements like "I think that," "chances are," and "it's unlikely that." What determines such beliefs? How do people assess the likelihood of an uncertain event or the value of an uncertain quantity?

According to cognitive psychologist Amos Tversky, people rely on a limited number of *heuristic* principles by which they reduce the complex tasks of assessing likelihoods and predicting values to simpler judgmental operations. A heuristic is a mental *shortcut* that allows people to solve problems and make judgments quickly and efficiently. These rule-of-thumb strategies shorten decision-making time and allow people to function without constantly stopping to think about their next course of action. Usually we find these mental operations useful, but they can lead to problems if we overuse them or rely on them too heavily. A better understanding of these heuristics and the biases to which they lead can improve judgment in situations of uncertainty—especially when that uncertainty involves risk, as it usually does.[4]

When considering the status quo, therefore, leaders do well to make sure it represents one and *only one* option. They put aside biases and improve the effectiveness of decisions when they ask: "If we weren't already doing this, would we *now* choose this alternative?" Often, leaders exaggerate the risk that selecting something else would entail, or they magnify the desirability of staying the course over time, forgetting that the future may well present something different.

Our fears, perceptions, and biases tell one story, but the facts tell a different one. As it turns out, the world, for all its imperfections, is in better shape than we might think. We have real problems, but when we spend our energies worrying about the future or feeling guilty about the past, we lose our focus and exhaust our abilities to solve problems, make high-caliber decisions, and take the necessary risks to grow and change. We see the aforementioned animals in the corporate jungle as creepy creatures we must avoid.

More than a century ago, Freud explained how we create these obstacles for ourselves. That is, the id, ego, and superego create a battlefield in our brains where the rational mind and emotional mind clash, just when we need them to make peace. They compete for control when we attempt to make risky decisions to effect transformative change. Successful changes, however, follow a pattern based on a mindset that tells us that change will bring improvement and most mistakes won't be fatal.

When our intellect and our emotions wage war, resilience and motivation suffer the consequences—the victims of a situation they didn't want in the first place. When this happens, we start to alter our beliefs, often developing a victim mentality, one characterized by pessimism and despair. How can a person tolerate ambiguity with such a mindset?

Revolutionary ideas constantly besiege leaders. Throughout history, everyone has been eager to help those in charge make smart, informed decisions about the future. Abraham Maslow and Douglas McGregor helped us understand the psychology behind human behavior. Deming, "the man who discovered quality" served as the prophet of the learning organization. We think of Peter Drucker as the founder of modern management and the inventor of the concept known as management by objectives.

All the theorists agree on one stark reality: It is possible for leaders to have a major impact on history, *if they are willing to take a chance on their ideas*. It won't happen automatically, however. Five psychological forces influence high-stakes decision-making: beliefs, cognition, emotions, motivation, and resilience. When leaders leverage all five, they develop a Disruptive Mindset—one that shapes resilience, recognizes that challenges aren't permanent; talented people can figure things out; and even failure isn't fatal. This mindset allows leaders to learn from past mistakes so they can move past them.

These leaders don't ignore, diminish, or deny the Black Swans, Gray Rhinos, or White Elephants. Instead, they trust their abilities to go on safari. They understand how human emotions help them function—or not. As systemic, discerning thinkers, they commit themselves to continuous learning and consistently remain open to new ideas without being naïve—all the while avoiding the trap of hubris. With optimism and a commitment to excellence, they steadfastly move ideas to action.

But our minds don't always work the way we think they do. We think we see ourselves as we really are and the world as it is, but we're actually missing quite a bit. In their book, *The Invisible Gorilla*, Christopher Chabris and Daniel Simons explained that intense focusing on a task can make people effectively blind, even to stimuli that normally attract attention. To prove their hypothesis, they constructed a short film of two teams passing basketballs, one team wearing white shirts, the other wearing black. The viewers of the film were instructed to count the number of passes made by the white team, ignoring the black-shirted players.[5]

Chabris and Simons meant to devise a task that was both difficult and completely absorbing. Halfway through the video, a woman wearing a gorilla suit appeared, crossed the court, thumped her chest, and moved on. The gorilla was in view for nine seconds. Many thousands of people have watched the video, but about half of them fail to spot the gorilla. The instructions to count passes and to ignore the players wearing black causes the blindness.[6]

The authors noted that the most surprising aspect of the experiment was viewers who failed to see the gorilla were initially sure that it hadn't been there. They couldn't imagine missing such a striking event. People who watch the video *without* the instructions about their task don't miss the gorilla, so they wonder how anyone could. The experiment proves two things: We can be blind to the obvious, and we are also blind to our blindness.

Nothing feels as painful as staying stuck where you don't belong, yet many, not realizing they're blind, confuse opportunism with dereliction of duty. When we don't prepare for the unexpected, we can't move quickly when surprises occur. Remember, you don't have to be faster than the bear. You just have to be faster than the others in the jungle.

HOW TO RELEASE TRAPPED VALUE

What happens when new and fast-improving technologies create opportunities to unleash untapped sources of revenue that have been trapped by market inefficiencies? That's the question Omar Abbosh, Paul Nunes, and Larry Downes asked when they began their research about how to turn disruption into opportunity. They introduced the term "wise pivot," a replicable strategy for harnessing disruption to survive, grow, and remain relevant into the future.

When companies pivot at the right time, they un-trap value that allows them to simultaneously reinvent their legacy, current, and new businesses. This allows them to turn the existential threats of today and tomorrow into sustainable growth. Leaders in these kinds of organizations have the courage to understand that a wise pivot strategy cannot be a one-time event. Instead, it should be a commitment to a future of perpetual reinvention, where one pivot follows the next and the next.[7]

Before these multiple pivots can occur, however, decision makers must understand how they trap value through their decisions and learn how to become the *disruptor* rather than the *disrupted* in any industry. It starts with an examination of their strategic principle, costs, customer responsiveness, and positive externalities.

What if leaders saw every disruption as an opportunity to innovate? Whether the opportunity is born of an entrepreneurial spirit or a response to a worldwide crisis, the ability to innovate during times of disruption can be the very thing that redefines the future of a given leader, company, or industry. Too often, however, companies trap value in the day-to-day management of their core activities and strategic forces. These artificial constraints, in turn, frequently raise unintended barriers to the company's growth and profitability.

The strategic forces of a given organization decisively affect its nature and direction, but they frequently inadvertently trap value, too. The categories of strategy components are numerous, but the first question an executive team would want to ask goes back to basics: "What are we about?"

Value starts with a strong strategic principle—a shared objective about what the organization wants to accomplish. The strategic principle guides the company's allocation of scarce resources—money, time, and talent.

The strategic principle doesn't merely aggregate a collection of objectives. Rather, this simple statement captures the thinking required to build a sustainable competitive advantage that forces trade-offs among competing resources, tests the soundness of particular initiatives, and sets clear boundaries within which decision makers must operate.

A well-thought-out strategic principle pinpoints the intersection of the organization's passion, excellence, and profitability, or in the case of

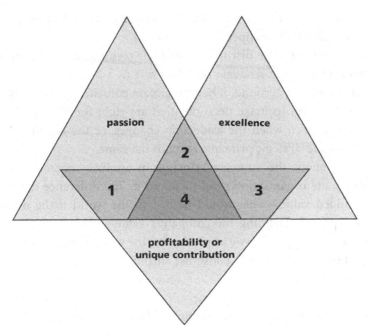

FIGURE 3.1
The Strategic Principle.

not-for-profit organizations, its unique contribution. As you can see from the graphic, success lies at the intersection of the three (see Figure 3.1).

Organizations that operate in section one often experience some short-term success, and star performers will find themselves drawn to work there—initially. But if the company doesn't offer the best of something and make money, competitors will soon surpass it.

Passion and excellence without profitability, or section two, won't even allow a short run. This undisciplined orientation—to do what you like and are good at—without consideration of the market, won't provide anything other than some short-lived fun, which should last right up until the time the bills come.

Section three offers a recipe for burnout. People can work hard at something they're good at and that makes them significant money, but they won't excel at it for long unless they feel some appetite for it. Star performers don't dip their professional toes in the water; they show up to make waves. If they don't feel passion for the work, they won't do either.

The sustained value of any company lies in section four, the intersection of passion, excellence, and profitability. These companies have high-quality products and services that consistently encourage them to develop newer and better value their competition can't match.

When companies face disruption—of their own making or in response to that of others—the strategic principle acts as a beacon that keeps the ships from running aground. It helps maintain consistency but gives managers the freedom to make decisions that are right for their part of the organization. Even when the leadership changes, or the economic landscape shifts, the strategic principle remains the same.

To think about the strategic principle in another way, consider the world *with* the organization versus *without* it. The difference defines the unique added value—what would be lost to the world if the organization disappeared. Defining the company's value-added principle, therefore, is the first step, *releasing* trapped value the second. Value can become ensnared by transition costs, consumer surplus, or a failure to create positive externalities.

Transition costs involve any charge, other than price, that a company suffers in trading products or services. *These costs* cover a wide range of fees including communication charges, legal fees, and search costs to find the best price, quality, and durability. We often refer to these as sunk costs—ones that can't be recovered. Companies incur transition costs when they recognize an opportunity but feel powerless in pursuing it because of existing processes, business models, or capabilities. These obsolete protocols and procedures, in turn, foster a culture of stagnation and compromise the development of a Disruptive Mindset. *Coordination costs*, a type of transition cost, trap value when technologies that could improve the entire ecosystem chiefly benefit only a small number of industry players.

Consumer surplus occurs when the price consumers pay for a product or service is less than the price they're willing to pay. This kind of trapped value exists when customers bear excessive costs that available technology could reduce. For instance, when incumbents ignore opportunities, new entrants rush in. Airbnb and eBay earned a combined $140 billion between 2004 and 2014 by facilitating transactions between consumers eager to buy and sell new and used goods for which there was previously no low-cost, easy-to-use market. These online platforms released nearly $1.4 trillion in value, most of it literally trapped in garages, attics, and storage lockers.[8]

Economists define an externality as the cost or benefit that affects a third party who did not choose to incur either. *Positive Externality* occurs when the consumption or production of a good causes a benefit. For example, homeowners who improve their homes and landscaping release trapped value by increasing property values for their neighbors. Companies release the trapped value of positive externality when they make decisions to protect the environment, their communities, and their industries. This leads to enhanced repute in an industry, which makes hiring easier and businesses more profitable.

We no longer consider disruption a once-in-a-career event or problem. It has become a constant cycle many have begun to call "the new normal." Only those leaders who quickly spot and leverage opportunities related to trapped value can close the gap between what's possible and what's likely.

While risk mitigation can often prove painful and feel unnatural, effective risk-management processes depend on it. The challenge to establishing a new risk culture depends on leaders encouraging project teams to kill the sacred cows of the status quo. Only then will they be willing to put aside their comfortable decision-making process to begin to think and talk about what could go wrong. This will demand that leaders encourage their teams to go beyond the checklists, procedures, and protocols that have become their security blankets to challenge, discuss, and debate best options for the changing environment. People will grouse and complain about *immediate* pain, but this pain will pale in comparison to the *eventual* pain of being stuck where you don't belong—and maybe you never did belong there in the first place.

SUPERFORECASTING

Leaders who have assumed the role of disruptors have learned to dramatically improve their organization's forecasting skills, but often the wisdom was born of pain. They have exposed just how unreliable their predictions—and the people making them—really were. Frequently a failed acquisition pulled back the curtain, but just as often the day-to-day processes of running a business distracted leaders from their most important decisions—the ones about where the company will be in the future. One of five things usually explains a failure to take a calculated risk:

1. Most people in most organizations can't recite the company's mission statement, much less articulate an ideal future state for the

organization, so they don't understand why a disruption should happen.

2. Leaders lose sight of the macro, concentrating too much on the micro—too much focus on tactics and activities and not enough on long-range goals.

3. People have an exaggerated concern about the disruptions that may happen in the short run instead of optimism about future gains and rewards. Leaders develop a propensity to fix current symptoms (to problem-solve), which only restores circumstances to the status quo, ignoring innovative decision-making.

4. Companies rely too heavily on big data and fail to hire those with *big judgment.* Those capable of superforecasting use data, logic, and analysis as the basis of their predictions, but they also gauge intangibles like biases, compatibility, and anticipated synergies.

5. Research suggests that usually groups make better decisions than individuals working alone. Groups take more risk because no one person "owns" the decision and the benefits or consequences of it. Yet leaders often fail to assemble and utilize the talent they have, or they create an environment where groupthink can lead to flawed forecasting.

When we allow blind spots and pain points to delude us, we also permit organizational biases to inhibit our ability to discuss risk and failure—and we trap value. When this happens, groups facing uncertain conditions often engage in *groupthink*, a tendency for group members to suppress their objections—no matter how valid—and fall in line. Groupthink happens most often when the leaders, internal or external, are overbearing or overly confident. These leaders inadvertently stand in the way of superforecasting, but they also impede the group's capacity to engage in logical predictions.

In 1972, social psychologist Irving Janis first identified groupthink as a phenomenon that occurs when decision makers accept proposals without scrutiny, suppress opposing thoughts, or limit analysis and disagreement. Teams behave this way because it feels safe, secure, and manageable. This exaggerated attempt to control risk frequently backfires, however. History provides numerous examples of this kind of flawed decision-making: Pearl Harbor, the Vietnam War, Watergate, the Challenger disaster, and the infamous Bay of Pigs invasion.

The Bay of Pigs invasion occurred shortly after John F. Kennedy took office in 1961. Those in Eisenhower's chain of command had conceived a plan to invade Cuba toward the end of his administration. Eisenhower had intended the invasion to touch off a nationwide Cuban uprising against Castro. When Kennedy took office, however, he abolished Eisenhower's Planning and Operation Coordinating Board, thereby eliminating the checks and balances inherent in Eisenhower's Council.

By financing and directing 1,500 anti-Castro Cuban exiles, the Central Intelligence Agency (CIA) hoped, under Kennedy's leadership, to overthrow Castro; it didn't work. On April 17, 1961, the landing of 1,453 Cuban exiles on the southwestern coast of Cuba turned, within 72 hours, into a complete disaster, resulting in the capture of 1,179 invaders and the death of the remaining 274.

Not only did the offensive fail, it also aggravated already hostile relations between the U.S. and Cuba, intensified international Cold War tensions, and inspired the Soviet Union to install missiles with nuclear warheads in Cuba the following year. Most historians agree that the participants who planned the invasion made some fundamental errors in judgment and predictions:

- Kennedy made the decision to invade based on the *theory* that the invasion would start a large-scale uprising, a miscalculation that proved later to be erroneous and costly.
- Although secrecy was mandated, Cubans living in Florida, American reporters, and presumably the Cuban government, knew about them.
- Members of the People's Revolutionary Movement, considered the most capable of the anti-Castro forces, did not join the invasion force, a decision that reduced the overall effectiveness.
- The U.S. did not show enough aggression in its support. Specifically, Kennedy refused the air support needed to protect the exiles.
- The U.S. created an impression of irresolution that contributed to the development of the Cuban Missile Crisis in October 1962.
- The original CIA plans called for an invasion that would produce the shock effect needed to cause the Cuban uprising. Although the CIA considered these uprisings essential to the success of the invasion, they went along with Kennedy's preferred "quiet landing" in order to have an invasion at all.

Why did this happen?

1. A high degree of cohesion and pressure to conform existed among CIA members, so they hesitated to challenge one another. The group *intentionally* kept dissenting opinions, when someone had the nerve to express them, from the President.
2. Members of the group thought affiliation with the President and top CIA and military leaders rendered them invulnerable. They shared the *illusion* that they were insulated because of the secrecy and presidential involvement, so they invented justification for their actions.
3. The decision makers sidestepped methodical research, planning, checks, and balances, focusing instead on the Machiavellian approach that overthrowing Castro justified any means to an end.
4. The group experienced a high degree of stress because they held little hope that they would find a better solution than the one advocated by the CIA. Incomplete and inaccurate intelligence caused the group to act hastily without thoroughly examining alternatives and risks.

Individual and organizational biases explain why so many leaders overlook or misread ambiguous threats. Rather than mitigating risk, leaders in these kinds of organizations actually *incubate* risk through *normalization of deviance*, a term American sociologist Diane Vaughan used to describe the process in which deviance from normal behavior becomes normalized in a corporate culture. This happens when decision makers learn to tolerate apparently minor failures and defects and treat early warning signs as false alarms rather than as alerts to imminent danger. If disasters like the ones mentioned can happen on a national or international level, what are the chances corporate leaders won't experience them if they fail to forecast intentionally and intelligently?

HOW TO DISRUPT FOR GROWTH

When should companies disrupt to grow? When times are good, and the business seems to be growing with little effort, why would leaders then decide to invest in new growth ventures? It seems so unnecessary, and investors frequently balk at the idea. When times are bad, and the company feels under siege from competitors, investors can't get enough profits to the bottom line fast enough, so why would they then decide to sail the ship into uncharted waters? Many leaders believe in the *concept* of disruptive innovation but remain skeptical about making it work—and it never seems like a good time to try.

Most leaders consider themselves innovative, but most of them show more adeptness at producing sustaining innovations—products and services that meet the demands of *existing* customers in *established* markets. Few leaders have introduced genuinely disruptive innovation—the kind that results in the creation of *entirely new ways of doing business.* The motivation to pursue innovation doesn't *seem* urgent, even when the facts tell a different story. In almost every industry, the most dramatic stories of growth and success involve leaders who launched a growth initiative from a platform of disruptive innovation.[9] Therefore, the only reasonable time to launch new growth initiatives—including acquisitions—happens when the core business is strong.

Disrupting for growth starts with superforecasting, but it can't end there. Instead, Disruptive Leaders base their decisions about the future on a process called *future-proofing. Future-proof,* the buzz term that describes a product, service, or technological system that will not need to be significantly updated as technology advances, had its origin in the technology and manufacturing arenas. People used it to describe the software or computer they would design to be used in the future, even when the technology changed.

Now, people use it to describe future offerings so that they can anticipate what's coming and develop methods to mitigate the negative effects the change might bring. In general, the term "future-proof," when used as a verb, refers to a process for making a product or service that will not become obsolete and will continue to have value into the distant future. For example, "What software should I buy to future-proof this system?"

People also apply the term to their children's education, flexibility, resourcefulness, and resilience: "How can I future-proof my child so that she can land on her feet even when jobs and industries change or disappear?" Similarly, it can be used as an adjective: "What future-proofing skills will this career choice entail?" Decision makers need to develop this future orientation in order to be disruptive without being disrupted. It serves as the basis for decisions about new customers, new markets, new products and services, and new business models.

Disruptive Leaders relentlessly focus on future customers and future needs for existing customers. That doesn't mean they ignore their *best* existing customers, but it does mean they shift from what *is* to what's *possible*, thereby lifting the strategy above departmental turf wars. It also means a strategy that focuses on future customers frees the company's assets and resources to pursue those customers, even when that means losing some existing customers who don't buy frequently or at high enough price points. Companies like Amazon and Netflix keep getting bigger because of this kind of orientation. They continually reinvest in the engine that drives disruptive growth.

To take the first step in finding new customers, determine which customers are unattractive or unavailable to the competition. That's what happened during the COVID-19 crisis. As governors forced malls and most brick-and-mortar retail shops to close, Amazon and Netflix sprang into motion and stepped into the fray. On March 2, 2020, a share of Amazon stock sold for $19,000. By the end of May, the stock sold for $500 more per share. Similarly, Netflix stock rose from $380 per share to $420 during the same time. Arguably, these two companies were poised and ready to disrupt because they had such strong histories of doing so. Therefore, when others felt disrupted by the virus, these two companies leveraged what they knew about disruption to respond to the new reality they faced—and profited in the process.

To develop a disruptive growth strategy, you need to systematically and intentionally weave a focus on future customers and their *yet-to-be-determined needs* into the fabric of the organization. General growth initiatives that pursue large obvious targets usually garner more support than disruptive ones. However, every major success story that exists today started as a small and poorly defined idea—just as the major disruptive opportunities of *tomorrow* currently seem insignificant and nebulous today.

In their research on disruptive businesses, Clay Christensen, Mark Johnson, and Darrell Rigby found that the success of disruptive strategies relies on leaders' ability to shape ideas that conform to a set of litmus tests:

- Does the innovation focus on customers who in the past have *not* been able to "do it themselves" for lack of money or skills? Services like online banking only serve a segment of their existing customers a bit more profitably and effectively, so they don't really disrupt, which means they don't move the needle on bringing in new business from future customers either. Conversely, online retail stockbrokers like E*Trade and Charles Schwab have the potential to create disruptive growth because they enable a new set of customers—day traders and those with relatively low net worth—to manage their own portfolios.

- Is the innovation aimed at customers who will welcome a simple product? Cramming disruption into established markets is both expensive and doomed for failure. Successful disruption targets customers who will welcome simple products.
- Will the innovation help customers do more easily and effectively what they are already trying to do? If an idea for growth is predicated on customers wanting to do something that hadn't been a priority in the past, it stands little chance of success.[10]

Spending too much on the wrong strategy in an attempt to get big fast, violating the litmus tests, and launching growth initiatives in an ad hoc manner when it's already too late to do so cooks up a recipe for pitfalls that causes a company to cease being disruptive and to feel the pain of being disrupted. Disrupting the basic business model of the company can do the same thing.

In 2012, *The Wall Street Journal* reported that Walmart was in the midst of the worst U.S. sales slump ever—at least until that year, posting its second straight year of declining sales. How did this happen to America's behemoth—a store that should have been thriving as customers looked for low-cost alternatives amid an economic downturn? They misstepped. To jumpstart lethargic growth and counter the rise of competitors, decision-makers veered away from the winning-formula mission: "Saving People Money So They Can Live Better." Instead, the world's biggest retailer raised prices on some items while promoting deals on others.

That wasn't the only change to its mission. A foray into organic foods didn't catch on with discount shoppers. Similarly, a push to sell trendy fashions and an attempt to cut clutter in stores to attract higher-income customers ended up alienating the company's traditional shoppers. The chain succeeded in attracting wealthier clientele but at the cost of its original customer base—those earning less than $70,000 a year, which made up 68% of its business. "The basic Walmart customer didn't leave Walmart. What happened is that Walmart left the customer," according to former Walmart executive Jimmy Wright.

The revolving door at corporate continued to spin as decision makers scrambled to go back to the mission that led to their success. Their attempts at disruption caused them to be disrupted but not more successful—at least not initially. Walmart stock sold for an average of $67 in 2012. By 2020, it sold for nearly twice that much in the throes of the COVID-19 crisis. Leaders at this retailer learned the hard way what to change and what to leave alone—what should be disrupted and what will merely cause the company to be disrupted.

Walmart made the mistake that time, but Pepsi, Continental Airlines, and United Airlines also fell into the trap of trying to be all things to all people—of ignoring how people will be better off with a change in a product or service. No one wants health food from Pepsi or designer clothes from Walmart. Everyone wants lower cost airlines, but unless the airline has done its homework, chances are it will end up in a low-cost war with Southwest and lose its uniform shirt. Walmart floundered, but it didn't sink. On the contrary, it sailed into profitable waters. At this writing, no one knows the fate of the airlines, even the major carriers. As Mark Twain (or was it John Billings?) once said, "It Ain't What You Don't Know That Gets You Into Trouble. It's What You Know For Sure That Just Ain't So." Leaders who aspire to grow will need to surround themselves with devil's advocates who will consistently and consciously challenge assumptions and anticipate consequences.

CONCLUSION

John Steinbeck said, "Change comes like a little wind that ruffles the curtains at dawn, and it comes like the stealthy perfume of wildflowers hidden in the grass." Change may come to individuals like that, but in most organizations, disruption is more like a tornado than a gentle wind. The COVID-19 pandemic disrupted business as usual, but there's nothing new about disruption. Demands of the marketplace, the accelerating pace of globalization, innovative technology, and new alliances all have created needs for leaders to help their people respond quickly and repeatedly to change. Responding to disruption will never be optional, but successful leaders should realize that disrupting for the greater good has now become mandatory.

NOTES

1 Taleb, N. (2010). *The Black Swan: Second Edition: The Impact of the Highly Improbable.* New York: Random House.

2 Wucker, M. (2016). *The Gray Rhino: How to Recognize and Act on the Obvious Danger We Ignore.* New York: St. Marin's Press.

3 Lam, J. (2019). "An Animal Kingdom of Disruptive Risks," National Association of Corporate Directors Blue Ribbon Commission.

4 Tversky, A. et al. (1973). Judgment Under Uncertainty: Heuristics and Biases. Oregon Research Institute prepared for Office of Naval Research Advanced Research Projects Agency.

5 Chabris, C. and Simons, D. (2010). *The Invisible Gorilla.* New York: Random House.

6 www.youtube.com/watch?v=vJG698U2Mvo.

7 Abbosh, O., Nunes, P., and Downes, L. (2019). *Pivot to the Future: Discovering Value and Creating Growth in a Disrupted World.* Hachette, New York: HYESHOM. P.22.

8 Abbosh, O., Nunes, P., and Downes, L. (2020). "Turning Disruption into Opportunity: How to Release Trapped Value." *Rotman Magazine.* Winter.

9 Christensen, C. (1997). *The Innovator's Dilemma: When New Technologies Cause Great Firms to Fall.* Boston, MA: Harvard Business School Press.

10 Christensen, C., Johnson, M., and Rigby, D. (2002). "Foundations for Growth." *MIT Sloan Management Review.* Spring.

4

The Influence of Conscious and Unconscious Bias on Risk-Taking

Every decision starts with a belief. That is, we base our decisions on what we know to be true—what we believe. Sometimes, however, we believe something that isn't true. Both intellectual and emotional, beliefs influence our behavior when facts and reason alone do not. Our early relationships, experiences, events, and situations create and influence our belief systems. However, when we fail to examine our beliefs and bring them to the conscious level, we run the risk that we will continue to base decisions on false or inaccurate inputs.

High-stakes decisions demand that we close the gap between what we *say* and what we actually *do*—the intersection of what we believe and how we behave. Then we can begin to understand how our unconscious beliefs create biases that shape our world view—and our mindset. When we actively examine our attitudes, biases, beliefs, and values, we take the requisite steps that build confidence that we can take a risk.

HOW DO WE FORM OUR BELIEFS?

Although he trained as a neurologist, Sigmund Freud felt a passionate draw to study human nature. As the "Father of Psychoanalysis," he developed therapeutic techniques for treating his patients, including a clinical method for treating psychopathology through dialogue between a patient and a psychoanalyst.

Any discussion of conscious and unconscious biases, therefore, should start with his "tip of the iceberg" theory. He constructed this theory to explain how an iceberg resembles the human man (I would say "mind," but to be accurate, Freud based most of his conclusions on his work with men). The smaller part of the iceberg that shows above the surface of the water represents the region of *consciousness* while the much larger mass below the water level represents the region of *unconsciousness*. This vast domain, Freud maintained, contains the urges, passions, repressed ideas, and feelings that exercise control over the conscious thoughts and actions of people, suggesting that limiting analysis to the consciousness is wholly inadequate for understanding human behavior.

In Freud's opinion, conflicts occur between the conscious and unconscious and among the components of each. People, therefore, continuously and inevitably find themselves in the grips of a clash between at least two opposing forces, making daily living a compromise that involves a dynamic balance of the forces. Freud identified three systems or components of the mind: the id, ego, and superego. Conflicts arise as the three systems of the mind compete for the limited amount of psychic energy available, energy that has its starting point in the instinctual needs of the individual.

The *id*, rooted in the biology of the individual, contains everything psychological that is inherited and present at birth, including instincts. The id, which Freud called a "seething cauldron," has no knowledge of objective reality; rather, it is a reservoir of psychic energy that consists primarily of urges, primitive desires, and unconscious sexual and aggressive instincts. This amoral part of the personality doesn't concern itself with the niceties and conventions of society. Rather, it operates on the "pleasure principle," a force that always strives to maximize enjoyment and minimize pain.

People do not exist in a vacuum, however, and fitting into any society demands the individual control impulses. The *ego* forms to provide direction for desires when a person's needs require interaction with the environment. The ego, therefore, develops to carry out the aims of the id by distinguishing between subjectivity and objectivity. The id concerns itself only with gratification, but the ego offers realistic thinking. The ego mediates between the visceral drives of the person and the conditions of the surrounding environment, providing a type of belief battlefield where the "armies" of the id and the superego continually clash.

The third system of personality, the *superego*, provides the moral part of the personality. It tries to inhibit the impulses of the id, especially sexual and aggressive ones. Concerned with what's right and wrong, the superego persuades the ego to substitute moralistic goals for realistic ones, to represent the *ideal* rather than the *real*, and to strive for perfection.

We can liken Freud's explanation of the three parts of the personality to the transactional analysis theory that each person contains a child (the id), an adult (the ego), and a parent (the superego). As we develop our belief systems, these various psychological processes frequently clash with one another, but usually the three work as a team under the administrative leadership of the ego.

Carl Jung joined Freud in the study of the unconscious but ultimately rejected many of Freud's ideas and created his own explanations of human behavior. Specifically, Jung viewed the personality, or psyche, as he called it, as several differentiated but interacting systems. While Freud stressed the inherited, instinctive forces that shape personality, Jung emphasized *social* and *environmental* factors. Freud theorized that the endless repetition of instinctual themes causes behavior, but Jung insisted destiny or purpose plays a role in a person's life.

According to Jung, not only do individual, ancestral, and racial history cause our behavior, but aspirations, purpose, and design do as well, combining with other forces to create the whole picture of the person. In other words, the racially influenced, collective personality selectively reaches into the world of experience and is, in turn, modified and elaborated by the experiences that it receives. The environment changes the individual, but predispositions also determine what an individual will become conscious of and respond to.

Another theorist, Karen Horney, emphasized sociocultural conditioning. In her judgment, unique *social* or *interpersonal* conditions, rather than biological make-up, have a more profound effect on an individual's development. As one of the few female theorists of the time, Horney stood apart because of her ability to add a different perspective on some of the male-dominated views. For instance, she criticized Freud's opinions about penis envy. Horney constructed a viewpoint that explained women do not suffer from penis envy, as Freud had stated. Rather, women justifiably envy the qualities associated with certain aspects of masculinity in most cultures. Since men created laws, religions, cultural norms, science, and art, women traditionally adapted themselves to the inferior status assigned to them.[1]

Philosopher Bertrand Russell claimed that *believing* is the most *mental* thing we do. Happiness expert Daniel Gilbert claimed it's also the most *social* thing we do. Gilbert contended that just as we pass along our genes in an effort to create people whose faces resemble ours, so too do we pass along our beliefs in an effort to create people whose minds think like ours. As he pointed out, every time we interact with another, we attempt to change the way that person's brain operates. Speakers, therefore, try to bring their listeners' beliefs about the world into harmony with theirs— and sometimes they succeed.

When does this successful transmission occur? According to biologist Richard Dawkins, the principles that explain why some genes are transmitted more successfully than others also explain why some beliefs are transmitted more successfully than others.[2] As Gilbert pointed out, we tend to transmit genes when they make us do the things that transmit genes. He called these genes "super-replicators." Even *bad* genes like the ones that make us prone to cancer, heart disease, and alcoholism can become super-replicators if they compensate for these costs by promoting their own means of transmission.

> For instance, if the gene that made orgasms feel delicious also left us prone to arthritis and tooth decay, that gene might still be represented in increasing proportions because arthritic, toothless people who love orgasms are more likely to have children than are limber, toothy people who do not.[3]

We can apply the same logic to the development of beliefs. If a specific belief has a property that facilitates its own transmission, then increasing numbers of people will tend to adopt that belief. False beliefs can become super-replicators, but *accurate* beliefs—ones that stand up to tests of logic—give us power, which makes it easy to understand why we readily transmit and develop them. The first step to understanding why we believe what we do is to raise our awareness of how we came to believe as we do. It all starts with self-perception.

BELIEFS ABOUT OURSELVES INFLUENCE MINDSET MORE THAN ANY OTHER FACTORS

Many people experience an *inner voice*, one that provides a running monologue throughout the day and into the night. This inner voice combines conscious thoughts with unconscious beliefs and biases and provides an effective way for the brain to interpret and process daily experiences. Known as *self-talk*, this internal chatter can be positive or negative—and sometimes at the same time.

We find this voice useful when it cheers us on and supports our best efforts. It helps us regulate our fears and bolsters our confidence. This voice takes on the vocal quality of our parents, teachers, coaches, and loved ones who told us our entire lives "You can do this!" I'm reminded of the lyrics to the country/western song, "I Ain't as Good as I Once Was":

I used to be hell on wheels,
Back when I was a younger man
Now my body says "Oh, you can't do this boy,"
But my pride says "Oh yes you can."

I still throw a few back,
Talk a little smack,
When I'm feeling bullet proof,
So don't double-dog dare me now,
Cause I'd have to call your bluff.

Although Toby Keith described positive self-talk in terms of being "bullet proof" and prideful, the average person's inner dialogue would arguably more reasonably resemble talking "a little smack." The greatest obstacle most face, therefore, doesn't involve reigning in this voice; it's silencing the negative one—the one that whispers, and sometimes yells—"You don't deserve this." Or "You can't do this." This same voice prevents us from taking prudent risks, even when the facts tell us we should.

When we suffer from weak self-esteem, low confidence, and lack of self-worth, we develop feelings of inadequacy that in turn trigger basic negative beliefs about ourselves. We begin to feel like imposters whom others will identify and humiliate. We begin to doubt ourselves, minimize our talents, and explain away our greatest accomplishments with "anyone could have done it" thoughts. These in turn lead to a fixed mindset that reminds us that we must assertively guard our accomplishments and arduously defend ourselves from any risk or threat. We cleave to the poverty mindset that seems safe and abandon an abundance mentality that would encourage us to innovate, grow, and change. Humans seem prone to negative self-talk, however, and to sweeping assertions like "I can't do anything right" or "I'm a complete failure."

Some people credit their inner critic with driving them to develop self-discipline and pushing them to recognize their weaknesses before others do. Over time, though, the negativity of a critical inner voice takes an emotional toll. Negative self-talk often does not reflect one's reality and can paralyze people into inaction and self-absorption.

Our negativity instinct also causes us to notice the bad more than the good. Three things are going on here: the *misremembering* of the past, often making it the "good old days" when it wasn't; the feeling that as long as things are bad, it's heartless to say they are getting better; and we are bombarded by negative news. (When was the last time someone reported all the airline flights that *didn't* crash?) Yet, when a plane does crash, it stays in the headlines for weeks and even months. Clearly, both inner and outer critics and negativity don't help us.

But the inner votary who worships our every thought and champions self-absorption doesn't do much better. Many leaders who hear this voice disproportionately function like victims of the so-called self-esteem movement that began in the 1960s and continues to this day. The movement quickly gained momentum, resulting in a 1990 decision of the California legislature to sponsor a report suggesting that self-esteem be taught in every classroom as a "vaccine" against social ills, such as alcohol abuse, drug addition, suicide, and teen pregnancy.

In 1986, former California state legislator John Vasconcellos established the "Task Force to Promote Self-Esteem and Personal and Social Responsibility." This prompted a three-year, 25-member investigation into the effect self-esteem has on society. The task force's records consist of *five and one-half cubic feet* of textual material and five cubic feet of audiovisual material covering the years 1987–1990. (A cubic foot is the space occupied by a cube with one-foot width, length, and height.) Cartoonist Garry Trudeau lampooned the effort in his *Doonesbury* comic strip, calling it "the embodiment of California wackiness" (see Figure 4.1).

Not everyone got the joke. The task force, which operated from 1987 to 1990, was a serious, or at least expensive, enterprise. It looked at the role of self-esteem in various areas, from crime and violence to academic failure and responsible citizenship. The commission's final report, released

FIGURE 4.1
Doonesbury Cartoon DOONESBURY © 2017 G. B. Trudeau. Reprinted with Permission of ANDREWS MCMEEL SYNDICATION. All Rights Reserved.

in 1990, became the best-selling state document of all time, selling 60,000 copies.[4]

Even without finding *causal* links between self-esteem and success, proponents of this movement advocated abolishing IQ testing, tracking in public schools, and class ranking. The movement gave birth to the everybody-gets-a-trophy mindset that society must adopt in order, advocates said, to avoid scarring underperforming children. Without question, a *correlation* between self-esteem and success exists, but no one proved *causality.* In other words, people who do well in school, sports, or business often exhibit signs they possess high self-esteem, but no proof exists that the high self-esteem *causes* the success. In fact, evidence exists to the contrary.

In 1996, researcher Roy Baumeister and his colleagues killed this sacred task-force cow in their study of genocidal killers, hit men, gang leaders, and other violent criminals. These researchers found that perpetrators with *unwarranted* high self-esteem became violent, meaning these reprobates *felt* good about themselves without actually *doing* anything laudable.

These findings suggest that if you teach unwarrantedly high self-esteem to children, without demanding praiseworthy behavior in return, confusion ensues. When these children confront the real world, and it tells them they are not as great as they have been taught, they lash out with violence.[5]

Might we accurately conclude that violence stems from the misbegotten notion that valuing how children feel about themselves more highly than how we value how they behave *causes* problems? Is it also possible that this everybody-gets-a-trophy mindset might also keep leaders from taking risks that might threaten the children's self-worth? Disruption becomes tougher when we confuse reality with what we think *ought* to be.

Rewarding smart risk-takers does not promote envy or enlarge the number of society's losers. Rather, it provides support for ideas that have shaped past progress—ideas that will aid future advancements so society wins. In other words, we become better educated, more productive, and healthier when we have the self-confidence to take prudent risks and the self-esteem to leverage the gains and learn from the losses.

Americans have stubbornly clung to the myth of egalitarianism— supremacy of the individual average person. We created the everyone-gets-a-trophy culture among our young, then it morphed into Cuckooland, a place where we shield losers who lose based on consequences from thinking they deserve to lose—a place where we think we should bar winners who win fairly from feeling confidence and pride.

Organizational success, the economic recovery, and global resurgence depend on something better—better, not just different. Success depends on a shift back to the notion that self-fulfillment, seductive though it may appear, must march in lockstep with a commitment to achievement.

Let's not totally disregard the importance of self-assuredness. Instead, let's understand it better and dispassionately evaluate the role it plays in engendering success. To start, we need to rediscover the intellectual confidence it takes to sort out and rank competing values. Fairness does not equal equality. Equal opportunity at the starting gun does not and should not guarantee equality at the finish line. Those who run through the tape at the finish line offer our greatest hope for thriving in the new economy.

Dr. Martin Seligman, the vanguard in the arena of positive psychology, pointed out that we have become depressed with a disorder of the "I," meaning we fail in our own eyes relative to the expectations we have for ourselves or that other people have for us. In a society in which individualism has become rampant, people too often believe they are the center of the universe. This dark side of self-esteem, therefore, makes individuals who fail inconsolable, and tough calls feel more threatening.

A second force, which Seligman called "the large we," formerly served as a force to buffer failure. When our grandparents failed, they had comfortable spiritual furniture to rest on—a safe place to land. They had their relationships with God, with a nation, with communities, and with a large extended family. Our faith in religions, community, the nation, and each other has all eroded in the past 50 years. The spiritual furniture we used to sit on has become threadbare, and the self-esteem movement has not helped us recover what we've lost.[6]

I'll call what we've lost "self-respect." When we have feelings of self-worth, not just entitlement, we can resist feelings of inadequacy and the imposter syndrome that makes us fear we'll be identified and humiliated—or fired. The greatest obstacle so many of my clients face involves the voice in their heads that murmurs—and sometimes screeches—words of discouragement. The reason? So many at the top don't solicit objective feedback from trusted advisors, people who have no other agenda than helping them improve. They get confused and either don't take the disruptive risks that would cause success, or they make imprudent ones only to rue them.

ESPOUSED VERSUS OPERATIONAL BELIEFS

When Ralph Waldo Emerson said, "What you are speaks so loudly I can't hear what you say," he captured the essence of what separates espoused beliefs (what we say we believe) from operating beliefs (the way we do things around here). But Emerson's observation omitted some other factors that influence beliefs such as habits, mental models, traditions—or the way we've *always* done things around here.

Our parents, teachers, ministers, peers, and social identity group memberships frame our experience of our world and create a lens through which we look to form conclusions and then judgments about others and ourselves. Many of the beliefs we have about ourselves develop early in life—derived from messages that have dropped into our unconscious and formed shortcuts, heuristics, and blind spots. We, in turn, go into the world and start dropping these missives into the psyches of others, creating an ongoing, nearly-impossible-to-stop cycle of communication, all the while influencing the conscious and unconscientious beliefs of others and building corporate cultures in the process.

When espoused and operational beliefs align, an ecosystem where people embrace risk as a means to attain excellence prevails amid fortitude and good judgment. But that doesn't always happen. More often, cultures evolve to reflect the beliefs senior leaders consider "correct." Over time, decision makers learn that certain beliefs work to reduce indecision and doubt in critical areas of the organization's functioning. As leaders continue to support these beliefs, and the beliefs continue to work, they gradually transform into an articulated set of more engrained beliefs, norms, and operational rules of behavior.

In his classic novel, *Anna Karenina*, Tolstoy stated that every happy family is alike, every unhappy family unhappy in its own way. Tolstoy meant that, to be considered happy, a family must succeed in critical respects: attraction between the husband and wife, agreement on key decisions related to child rearing, money, and other vital issues. Failure in any one of these essentials can doom a family, even if its members have all the other ingredients needed for happiness.

From Tolstoy came "The Anna Karenina Principle," a belief positing that in order for an organizational endeavor to succeed, the people involved must avoid every possible deficiency, making success more elusive than failure—a perfect storm of contributors. The absence of only *one* of these significant contributors precludes the positive, desirable, or worthy. Conversely, we have a banquet of options for harming an organization: greed, inadequate leadership, poor performance, faulty decision-making, external pressures, etc., making the road to failure wide and varied.

In nature and in business, myriad and unlimited reasons exist for failure—opportunities for success remain more limited. Missing a target is easy, hitting it more difficult. None of this implies that leaders should pursue perfection. On the contrary, perfection will continue to serve as the arch-enemy of both success and excellence. Successful change requires a mindset shift—a new way of looking at the organization's environment—a realization that success has more to do with how a company makes money than how it clings to its "culture."

Gone are the days of *describing* both the espoused and operational beliefs of leaders, here to stay times of *prescribing* what must happen for success. A new recipe for results has emerged, but not everyone has lost a taste for the old one.

In most organizations, leaders give considerable thought to espoused values. These values may appear on a plaque in the foyer or on a mouse pad, but successful leaders also model them. Values play an important role in forming an organization's culture because senior leaders agree, "This is the way we do things around here."

Unconscious assumptions remain more mysterious, lying below the surface, undetected but ready to influence outcomes both positively and negatively. In damaged organizations, unconscious biases commonly contradict the espoused values, causing confusion within and without the company. They also engender mistrust, suspicion, and, eventually, the loss of customers and star performers.

Operational beliefs describe the principles and standards that guide a leader's ethical and business decisions. When asked to compose a list of their organization's values, leaders typically mention integrity, quality, customer satisfaction, and enhanced shareholder value. While laudable, which of these would a successful company *not* value since success demands each of them? A list of ideals *any* organization would embrace doesn't really distinguish a success-driven company from any other, and it doesn't get at the core of what might compromise a particular entity's success. Tolstoy commented on marriages; we can make the same observation about organizations: successful organizations seem alike; each unsuccessful one fails in its own way.

Excellence demands that beliefs address the tempests that can trigger failure and provide a compass for navigating uncharted seas, even at high cost. Instead of writing laudable values on a plaque in the foyer, successful leaders *live* their corporate beliefs and expect others to do the same since these beliefs serve as criteria for making business decisions.

Actions—the tough calls involved in running any organization—don't speak louder than words. Frequently, "actions" don't even whisper because they take place between the two ears of senior leaders. However, most people don't consider decision-making the most important action leaders take. Decisions—good, bad, seen, or unseen—serve as the link between the leader's beliefs and the results the organization will enjoy or rue. When we trace tragedy and regret back to their roots, we find ourselves lamenting a bad decision, or noticing, in retrospect, a decision leaders didn't even realize they had made or failed to make. When leaders create an environment where words and actions operate in harmony, however, an almost magical alchemy takes place.

Alchemy, the medieval forerunner of chemistry, addressed the transformation of matter—attempts to convert base metals into gold by using the Philosopher's Stone or efforts to confer youth and longevity through the Elixir of Life. Alchemy involved liberating parts of the cosmos from temporal existence and achieving perfection—gold for metals and longevity, immortality, and redemption for people.

In organizations, alchemy involves transforming the status quo (the base metals) into the golden ideas of improvement—not simply different ideas but better ones. From this change comes innovation, which stands squarely at the heart of organizational learning—with rigidity, caution, and fear as its arch-enemies. Fear causes us to build silos that serve as our fortresses. When we fear, we go into protection mode and become risk-averse.

Espoused beliefs start with an individual's perception of right and wrong, someone's sense of what *ought* to be as opposed to what *is*. When outcomes prove the individual correct, and others observe this, they create shared beliefs or shared assumptions that the same course of action will work into the future.

For example, the leader of a sales group advocates a team approach to sales. She revamps the compensation package to reward team behavior. Then everyone sees sales soar. The leader's espoused value of the importance of teamwork quickly turns to a shared assumption that teams, rather than individuals, should work to increase business. Over time, as newcomers adopt a team approach, the espoused value gradually morphs into an operating belief—but only if the approach continues to meet sales demands. A transformation occurs: habits form, mindsets evolve, all giving birth to a tradition, a kind of track record.

Several years ago, I spent a day at the Air Force Academy as part of the National Security Forum annual reunion. From the time our group entered the Academy grounds until we left, we saw evidence of the cadet honor code: "We will not lie, steal, or cheat nor, tolerate among us anyone who does."

This is not some slogan that somebody put on the plaque in the foyer of the company. It's not an arbitrary list of "values" that the company aspires to live by but never quite achieves. Nor is this a generic menu of all things good that we value: communication, teamwork, diversity, daily flossing.

This statement defines the code the cadets have committed to uphold. They didn't go on a two-day retreat to cook this up and then ignore it thereafter. Rather, in this simple statement that has long stood as the Academy's Honor Code, the cadets and their counterparts at the other service academies have expressed a willingness to expel anyone who violates it, whether that person is average or exceptional. No exceptions.

The first part of the code seems straightforward—the second part more complicated. The cadets state that they will not tolerate anyone who violates the code. That means that if they find someone among them has lied, cheated, or stolen, they will alert the authorities—not the college's administrators but members of the Cadet Honor Committee. Failing to do so endangers the cadet who knew of the violation.

Cheating poses the biggest threat to the service academy student body. As students in a highly competitive environment, they feel tremendous pressure to succeed academically. Those who attempt shortcuts, however, usually find expulsion, not success.

Corporate America has much to learn from the cadets at our military institutions. They experience no cognitive dissonance about core beliefs versus espoused beliefs—they are one in the same. Perhaps it's naïve to assume all the economic woes of the U.S. could be solved with a simple dedication to honorable behavior, but it's a start.

WYSIATI: WHAT YOU SEE IS ALL THERE IS

In 2002, Daniel Kahneman received the Nobel Prize in Economic Sciences for his pioneering work with Amos Tversky on decision-making. They established a cognitive basis for common human errors that arise from heuristics and biases. In his groundbreaking book, *Thinking, Fast and Slow*, Kahneman coined the term WYSIATI to explain the remarkable asymmetry between the ways our minds treat available information and information we do not have. He noted that the dominance of conclusions over arguments is most pronounced when emotions are involved.

Another psychologist, Paul Slovic, proposed the concept of *affect heuristic* that explains why people let their likes and dislikes determine their beliefs about the world. As both found, our emotional attitudes cause us to develop beliefs about the risks of our high-stakes decisions. For instance, I don't understand why anyone would *ever* voluntarily ride a motorcycle. In my belief system, the risks of doing so are so high and the benefits negligible. Some of my male friends disagree. Even though they have read the same data about motorcycle fatalities that I have, they consider the benefits far greater than the risk—and the risks don't get much higher than death. Consequently, two human phenomena surface simultaneously. We make our decisions based on WYSIATI reasoning and give disproportionate weight to our preferences.

We cannot help dealing with the limited information we have as if it were all there is to know—unless we really try. We have an almost unlimited ability to ignore our ignorance, so overcoming WYSIATI demands the discipline to seek more information—especially when we think we have enough and when we let our preferences guide us. Because of WYSIATI, only the evidence at hand counts, and the subjective confidence we have in our opinions reflects the coherence of the story we construct in our heads. As Kahneman noted:

> We are confident when the story we tell ourselves comes easily to mind, with no contradiction and no competing scenario. But ease and coherence do not guarantee that a belief held with confidence is true. The associative machine is set to suppress doubts and to evoke ideas and information that are compatible with the currently dominant story. A mind that follows WYSIATI will achieve high confidence much too easily by ignoring what it does not know.[7]

When an organization faces a significant decision, especially one involving disruption, senior leaders do well to frame the opportunity for themselves and others. Mental frames determine how we view a situation and how we interpret it. Conscious and unconscious biases play a role in constructing these frames, sometimes to our benefit, often to our detriment.

We improve our risk-taking abilities when we don't automatically accept frames—ours or anyone else's. When we ask, "Is this really the issue?" we force ourselves to get to the core of the problem without being distracted by symptoms, indications, causes, or effects.

People who understand the role framing plays in WYSIATI thinking also understand how both exert influence. They have learned that establishing the framework within which others will view the decision is tantamount to determining the outcome.

WYSIATI, unconscious biases, and heuristics all influence the development of a Disruptive Mindset—but not always for the better. Because we are all susceptible to these decision-making experiences and averse to mental effort, we tend to make decisions as problems arise instead of proactively looking into the future. We often have neither the inclination nor the mental resources to enforce consistency on our preferences, and our preferences are not magically set to be coherent.

Global unconscious bias and inclusion expert Dr. Helen Turnbull warned against the dangers of these kinds of "blind spots" in decision-making. As she noted, we have learned in the past decade or so how to be politically correct—a widely accepted and extolled approach devised to help us keep from offending one another. But as Turnbull noted, all political correctness did was take issues and push them under the table. From that position, "leakage" occurs when unspoken attitudes and beliefs drive behaviors, even when we try to mask the reasons for the behavior. In other words, most people recognize when they *consciously* dislike others, but if they don't pay attention to their *unconscious* shortcuts, they create the blind spots that cause them to act in ways that don't benefit anybody.[8]

While heuristics can reduce the burden of decision-making and free up cognitive resources, they can also prove costly when they cause people to miss critical information or act on unjust biases. When we don't discipline ourselves to hear differing opinions and to conscientiously consider alternatives, we act impulsively, make rash decisions, or fail to take appropriate risks. Both compromise innovation and growth and put us on the path to bad habits.

HOW HABITS INFLUENCE BELIEFS AND VICE VERSA

Too often discussions of attitudes, values, and beliefs center on the person, making us blind to the power of the *situation*: marketing specialists advocate finding the right psychographic for a product; psychologists talk about finding the person who is ready to quit smoking; human resource managers focus on getting the right people on the bus; and change experts encourage us to classify people according to the readiness to accept change.[9] As a consultant who specializes in succession planning and C-suite selection, I admit I have fallen into this trap, too.

But Stanford psychologist Lee Ross did not. Instead, he developed *The Fundamental Attribution Error* theory by surveying dozens of studies in psychology and noting that people have a systematic tendency to ignore the situational forces that shape other people's behavior. As Ross pointed out, the error lies in our inclination to attribute people's behavior to *the way they are* rather than to *the situation they are in*.[10] So often, something that looks like an attitude problem is really a situation problem.

Therefore, tweaking the environment frequently alters beliefs, which in turn makes the right behavior easier and the wrong behavior a little less so. For example, last year I coached an executive in the construction industry who was having trouble prioritizing, which fueled his anxiety. He simply wasn't getting things done.

I asked Pete to walk me through a typical day so I could help him identify when he was creating a situation that fueled the anxiety. He said he opened email first thing in the morning, which immediately triggered apprehension. So, first thing out of the gate, Pete felt overwhelmed, which caused him to have trouble prioritizing, which caused him to lose control of his day, which caused him to miss deadlines.

Pete said, "That's just the way I am," but I didn't let him get away with that. Instead, I asked him to change his situation by deconstructing success he'd had previously. He admitted that in the past he had created folders for non-critical emails that he'd handle on certain days and certain times. In other words, he took control and changed his situation, which changed his beliefs about what's important, which changed his habits. Some psychologists might call this "self-manipulation." I choose to call it "self-regulation." Either way, changing the situation can lead to the self-awareness that drives behavior change.

As Pete demonstrated, the environment acts in subtle—and sometimes conspicuous—ways to reinforce or deter our habits. We are incredibly sensitive to the environment and the culture—to the norms and expectations of the communities we choose. Also, he reminds us that if what we're doing doesn't work, we should quit doing that and get ourselves off behavior autopilot.

In 1892, American philosopher William James wrote, "All our life, so far as it has definite form, is but a mass of habits." We develop these habits because the brain constantly seeks ways—such as biases, heuristics, and short cuts—to save effort. Our early relationships, experiences, events, and situations create and influence our belief systems. Sometimes, however, people consciously pursue groups such as Alcoholics Anonymous to help them change their beliefs and habits. Similarly, we deliberately look for employment in companies that seem to match our belief systems (or at least don't cause us cognitive dissonance by conflicting with our values). Sometimes our habits don't match those of everyone else in these organizations, but we develop routines that create truces among disparate groups and individuals.

When we fail to examine our beliefs and biases and bring them to the conscious level, we run the risk that we will continue to base decisions on false or inaccurate inputs. We end up in situations that cause us to form unhealthy habits and routines, which create a downward spiral of flawed risk-taking. We don't have to do things this way; we just usually do. So, what can we do to disrupt belief systems, change habits, and improve decisions?

1. Kill sacred cows. Just because you've always believed something, it doesn't mean you have to continue to believe it.
2. Create new situations. Instead of creating an uphill battle for yourself every day, design a steep downhill slope and give yourself a push. Remove friction from the trail, and scatter around many signs to let you know you're succeeding.
3. Get new habits and routines. Follow Pete's lead and deconstruct your personal and professional successes. When you've changed your behavior in the past, what did you do?
4. Reduce cognitive dissonance. People don't like to act in one way and think in another. So once a small step has been taken, and people begin to act in a new way, it will be increasingly difficult for them to dislike the way they're acting. Similarly, as people begin to act differently, they'll start to think of themselves differently, and as their identity evolves, it will reinforce the new way of doing things.

CONCLUSION

We may understand *intellectually* we make better decisions when the chasm between what we say and how we behave narrows, but that doesn't always guarantee success. Too often our unconscious beliefs conspire against us. They create biases that shape our world view and our mindset. When we *actively* examine our mental and emotional shortcuts, we take the requisite steps that build confidence that we can take a risk and truly disrupt the-way-we've-always-done-things-around-here strategies.

When people wrongly believe that nothing is improving, they may conclude that nothing they have tried so far works and lose confidence in things that actually do work. Too often clients want to tell me everything they have done that didn't work and fail to mention all the efforts that moved the needle, even just a little.

―――――――――

NOTES

1 Ryckman, R. M. (1985). *Theories of Personality*. Monterey, CA: Brooks/Cole Publishing Company.
2 Dawkins, R. (1976). *The Selfish Gene*. Oxford: Oxford University Press.
3 Gilbert, D. (2006). *Stumbling on Happiness*. New York, NY: Vintage Books. P. 237.
4 (California task force) www.oac.cdlib.org/findaid/ark:/13030/kt8b69r98n/.
5 Baumeister, R., Smart, L., and Boden, J. (1996). "Relation of Threatened Egotism to Violence and Aggression: The Dark Side of High Self-Esteem." *Psychological Review*. 103, no. 1, P. 5.
6 Seligman, M. (1990). *Learned Optimism*. New York, NY: Free Press.
7 Kahneman, D. (2011). *Thinking, Fast and Slow*. New York, NY: Farrar, Straus and Giroux. P. 209.
8 Turnbull, H. (2016). *The Illusion of Inclusion: Global Inclusion, Unconscious Bias, and the Bottom Line*. New York, NY: Business Expert Press.
9 Heath, C. and Heath, D. (2010). *Switch: How to Change Things When Change is Hard*. New York, NY: Penguin Random House.
10 Ross, L. (1977). "The Intuitive Psychologist and His Shortcomings: Distortions in the Attribution Process." *Advances in Experimental Social Psychology* (vol. 10). New York, NY: Academic Press.

5

Aptitude Always Outranks Experience

We know our mindset serves as more than the sum of its neuronal connections. It links us to external reality while creating our sense of who we are and what makes us different from everyone else. It contains both objective (I took Algebra in high school) and subjective (Algebra was my least favorite class) components. My brain remembers the rules for balancing equations but also recalls the smell of the Atlantic Ocean I visited for the first time the week after completing the course. You will find the mindset housed in the brain, but it extends well beyond as it constantly engages with the brains of other people, the environment, and the culture. The physical components of the human mind alone do not adequately explain the human experience. Neurons may provide the material for human consciousness, but they alone don't create it. We also possess souls that no computer can ever replicate.

The soul-searching process of risk-taking involves more than evaluating what we see and hear: it's a biological process—part physiological, part psychological, and part contextual—but not always rational. Those who have the right mindset for successful disruption reduce the risk of very human cognitive biases and decision traps. They think systemically. Both discerning and curious, they remain open to new ideas without being naïve, and they avoid the trap of hubris. They weigh tradition while challenging themselves to remain open to new ideas. They steadfastly evaluate new information as they discipline themselves to simultaneously process information from a variety of sources as they deal with multi-dimensional issues.

CONVENTIONAL WISDOM IS NEITHER CONVENTIONAL NOR WISE

Why don't we throw a fire extinguisher to someone who's drowning? Conventional wisdom certainly informs us that we need fire extinguishers in many emergencies and that every one household should have several, yet you don't hear of lifeguards throwing them. Why? Sometimes we figure out that every solution doesn't apply to every problem.

We know conventional wisdom includes the body of ideas and explanations generally accepted as true by experts in a given field, but common sense (which isn't all that common) dictates we can't always solve new problems in old ways. We also define conventional wisdom as the ideas so accepted that they go unquestioned. Those who wish to innovate, change, and disrupt, however, learn to question at a three-year-old's level of commitment, continuously asking, "Why?"

That's what medical researchers have done through the ages. Before the discovery of insulin, diabetes led to death. Doctors knew that sugar worsened the condition of diabetic patients and that the most effective treatment demanded putting the patients on extremely strict diets with sugar intake, and food in general, kept to a minimum. Researchers developed the mantra: "The less food, the more life." At best, this treatment caused patients to live a few extra years, but it never saved them. In some cases, the harsh diets even caused patients to die of starvation. Most medical breakthroughs started with a smart person asking "Why? Why isn't this working? What else might work? What challenges convention?" Whether attempting to put a man on the moon or solve medical problems, smart people never stop questioning the status quo.

That's what scientists did to develop a cure for diabetes. Dr. Frederick Banting, a Canadian physician, developed a deep interest in diabetes after reading an article in a medical paper on the pancreas. The work of other scientists had indicated that the lack of a protein hormone secreted in the pancreas caused diabetes. They named this protein "insulin."

Determined to investigate the possibility of extracting insulin from the pancreas, Banting discussed possibilities with various people, including Professor John Macleod. Macleod didn't think much of Banting's theories, but Banting managed to convince him that his idea merited further research. In 1921, Macleod gave Banting a laboratory with a minimum of equipment, ten dogs, and a research assistant named Charles Best.

After Banting and Best discovered insulin and proved it could save lives, they encountered trouble finding ways to purify and extract it. Scientists James Collip and Duncan Graham joined the group and a tumultuous commitment to challenge conventional wisdom pursued.

Amid high drama and posturing, doctors admitted Leonard Thompson, a 14-year-old diabetic boy, to Toronto General Hospital on December 2, 1921. During all this tumult, the science continued on two tracks—research and clinical. On January 23, doctors began injecting the child with the new extract. As the boy had been near death, those involved saw his recovery as nothing short of miraculous.

Very soon after the discovery of insulin, the medical firm Eli Lilly started large-scale production of the extract. Two years later, the company began producing enough insulin to supply the entire North American continent, which positioned Lilly as one of the world's major pharmaceutical manufacturers.

The story of this miraculous discovery, that began with a team of Canadian virtuosos who fought each other both literally and figuratively, has a happy ending; but few involved would have characterized the experience as pleasant, much less happy. People seldom find questioning the status quo and the inevitable conflicts that ensue enjoyable. The rewards came from the keen dedication of the team members to accomplish the daunting goal of controlling the then-killer disease of diabetes. Two things allowed the research to become a reality: the exceptional cognitive abilities of the scientists and the Disruptive Mindset of their leader, Dr. Macleod. Had either been absent, countless lives would have been wasted until a strong leader could have surfaced to orchestrate the efforts and conflicts of this team of virtuosos.

The BP oil spill of 2010, the worst in U.S. history, offers further evidence that convention is not always wise. Conventional wisdom would have us believe that the more information a decision maker has, the better. Coast Guard Admiral Thad Allen, the incident commander, disagreed. Allen estimated that he received 300–400 pages of emails, texts, and messages every day. We will never know whether less information would have allowed officials to figure out sooner how to cap the well, but Allen admitted to reporters that the torrent of data might have contributed to the mistake of failing immediately to close off air space above the gulf—a situation that led to eight near-mid-air collisions.

As Allen learned, every piece of incoming information presents a choice about what to do: pay attention, react, ignore, or prioritize. When people face a plethora of options, however, they too often opt to make no decision at all. Conventional wisdom tells us we want all available data, because we fear that one piece of missing information may prove critical, but frequently an overabundance of information leaves us feeling we have fewer options—and we feel less satisfied with the choices we make. Our fear of criticism or loss of control causes the proliferation of choices to create paralysis when the stakes are high and the information complex. As Allen demonstrated, the booming science of risk-taking is showing us that the more information we have, the more likely we will engage in objectively poorer choices—ones we often regret.

Although we say we prefer more information, in fact more can be "debilitating," argued social psychologist Sheena Iyengar in her book, *The Art of Choosing*. As she noted, we compare bundles of information when we make decisions. Therefore, decisions become harder as the amount of information we must juggle grows.[1] In recent years, businesses have offered more and more choices to cater to individual tastes. For simple items like mustard or socks, this may not pose a problem, but the proliferation of choices can create paralysis in high-stakes situations laden with complex information. More information may lead to objectively better choices, but we'll often feel less satisfied with the decisions.

The quantity of information isn't the only thing that stands at cross-purposes with our risk-taking. The *rate* at which we receive information can also knock the brain for a loop. The ceaseless influx of data trains us to respond instantly, sacrificing accuracy and thoughtfulness to the false god of immediacy. Clifford Nass, the author of *The Man Who Lied to His Laptop*, noted we've been trained to prefer an *immediate* decision, even if it's a bad one, to a later decision that's better. In business, I'm seeing a preference for the quick over the right, in large part because so many decisions have to be made, and the notion that the fast decision is better has become the norm.

We know the brain is hardwired to notice change over stasis, and recency often eclipses quality. So, we end up paying exaggerated attention to information that challenges tradition, and we fixate on the last thing we heard.

Our minds constantly struggle to decide what to ignore and what to consider. Sometimes it's much easier to look for more and more information instead of patiently considering how it all fits together. Jean-Paul Sartre once said, "Everything has been figured out, except how to live." I would add that the reason we haven't figured out how to live is because we haven't figured out when to take a chance—even on ourselves.

Helen Reddy assured us "wisdom's born of pain," and the ancient Greek tragedian Aeschylus observed, "He who learns must suffer. And even in our sleep pain that cannot forget, falls drop by drop upon the heart, and in our own despair, against our will, comes wisdom to us by the awful grace of God." Billy Joel assured us "You're not the only one who's made mistakes, but they're the only thing that you can truly call your own." Perhaps they were all wrong. Maybe wisdom most often comes from learning from our success and joy.

HOW SMART IS SMART ENOUGH?

In the early 1900s, American psychologist Lewis Terman recognized the importance of intelligence when he pioneered the Stanford-Binet and other IQ tests, using children as many of his study participants. In his opinion, nothing about an individual mattered as much as intelligence, except morals. I agree with Terman, with one addition. Integrity and intelligence will win many games, but usually they won't be enough. Winning players—the ones who will define the game for everyone else—need reasonably high IQs *and* a Disruptive Mindset.

When people possess a Disruptive Mindset, they have a positive response to new and different information—an abundance mentality. They want to grow because they believe they will always have enough of what they need, and usually they will have more than enough. They allow excitement, curiosity, passion, and achievement-drive to guide their risk-taking. Most importantly, they control their own fears and try to mitigate the negative emotions of others.

People with a Disruptive Mindset see the world differently from those who have a scarcity mentality. People with a poverty mindset believe their basic qualities, like intelligence, are simply unchanging traits. These people spend their time *documenting* their talents instead of *developing* them. They also believe that talent *alone* creates success—without effort.

Smart risk-takers consider their brains the starting point but realize they will develop their basic abilities only through dedication and hard work. This view creates a love of learning and the resilience essential for great accomplishments. Welcoming and teaching a growth mindset creates motivation, increases productivity, and enhances relationships.

If people have a Disruptive Mindset, how high does their IQ need to be for them to successfully disrupt the status quo and venture into uncharted seas? As a frame of reference, most successful professional football players are big guys, but beyond a certain weight, you don't see increased skill or excellence. Like the size of NFL players, intelligence has a threshold. You must be smart enough to do the job well—but not appreciably smarter. Some studies say an IQ of 115, which most people typically need to earn a master's degree, will be smart enough to succeed in most management positions. I don't agree.

I don't administer IQ tests, but I do cognitive assessments that allow me to infer the IQ of C-suite executives and business owners. The clients I've assessed have IQs higher than 115—usually in the 115–130 range. Intellect above 115 allows for abstract thinking, an essential for strategy formation and disruptive decisions. However, I've worked with extremely intelligent people who were so caught up in the idea that their brains should matter more than anything else that they were nearly un-coachable. They had the brains but not the mindset to succeed.

I'm thinking of Sam, a risk expert I coached several years ago. Sam blew the top off every cognitive assessment I administered. When I gave him feedback, nothing surprised him. Sam knew he was the smartest guy in the building.

As I explained to Sam, his boss, the CEO, wanted him to quit giving so much detail in his analysis and just say, "Here's what I recommend." The boss hired Sam because he's a specialist. He didn't hire him to serve as a private tutor.

Sam took offense. He wanted to take every opportunity to "show his work," as we used to say in Algebra class, to the CEO and others on the leadership team. I tried to help Sam develop a three-step process for giving information that would take him 30 seconds. He resisted.

Sam's smarter than I am, so why should he listen to me? And he's smarter than the CEO, so why should he adjust his behavior to his boss's preferences? He found the entire system so unfair. Why couldn't everyone just recognize his brilliance and let him decide how to use it?

Things didn't end well for Sam. He continued with his habits for several years until he decided to violate company protocol and visit some unauthorized websites on the company computer—probably the dumbest mistake any of my clients has ever made. (Imagine dinner at Sam's house the night he tried to explain to his wife why he got fired.) Not only did Sam think he should make his own rules, he also concluded the company's rules didn't apply to him. It was a bad day when HR had to march Sam's brains and experience out the door for an integrity violation. Sam had the brains but not the ability to use them wisely.

Twenty-five years after his original research with the gifted "Termites," his name for the children he studied, Lewis Terman discovered that persistence and the ability to set goals separated the more successful from the less successful members of the original group. In other words, you have to start with enough brains to do the job, but intelligence alone won't define success.

Decades later, Angela Duckworth's research, which she described in her book, *Grit*, clearly showed that *persistence* matters, too. Her early eye-opening stints in teaching, business consulting, and neuroscience led her to hypothesize that what really drives success is not genius, but a unique combination of passion and long-term perseverance. As she noted, intellect is important but without grit, results won't be as good.

A Disruptive Mindset—one that shapes grit—recognizes that challenges aren't permanent; talented people can figure out solutions; and even failure isn't fatal. The Disruptive Mindset allows leaders to learn from past missteps and helps them move past them, so people and organizations can thrive. They understand what Oscar Wilde meant when he wrote, "Experience is the name everyone gives to their mistakes." If you hire smart people who demonstrate that they have the right mindset, how can success *not* follow?

WHY CURIOSITY MATTERS

I finished my doctoral research in 1998 at what was then called the Fielding Graduate Institute (now Fielding Graduate University). The week of my graduation, I had the honor of meeting Dr. Barnett Pearce, the coauthor of the *Coordinated Management of Meaning Theory*. This communication theory posits that three main principles govern the transmitting of information: There are multiple social worlds; these social worlds are made in interactions and through conversations with others; and we are all active agents in the making of social worlds.

Barnett had just joined the faculty at Fielding and entered as I exited the school. I was heartsick that I wouldn't have the chance to work with this great thinker who already commanded two pages of the literature review in my doctoral dissertation, but I was grateful that I had had the opportunity to talk to him about his work.

During our first meeting, the ever affable and avuncular Barnett immediately turned our conversation to me and asked me how I felt as I prepared to take the stage for graduation. I admitted that I felt humbled. Even though I had immersed myself in scholarly pursuits for the previous four years, on the day of my graduation I felt like an imposter who had only begun to learn all there was to know. Barnett admitted he had felt the same way on the day he graduated with his doctorate. He said as he walked through the library of his school, he literally wept that the books there represented how much remained unlearned. He also assured me my admission that I had learned so little and had so much still to learn qualified me for graduation. On the day of my own graduation, this theorist and philosopher introduced me to the value of curiosity—the cornerstone of both effective learning and risk-taking. That day I also realized intellectual humility is the ability to acknowledge what we don't know and to eagerly set new learning goals.

Since then, I have continued to be curious about curiosity. When I help clients with C-suite selection or succession planning, I assess curiosity by measuring candidates' tendencies to seek intricate solutions and abstract thinking. The candidates I recommend are attentive, involved people who show an interest in learning about a diversity of things. They have a track record for invention, the capacity for originality of thought, and the motivation to develop novel solutions. They value new ideas and evidence an interest in pursuing topics in depth, regardless of their difficulty or intricacy.

I also measure risk-taking tendencies but value high scores only when I see exceptional cognitive abilities and curiosity. Neither impulsivity nor recklessness impresses me, however, and an extreme score on either often causes me to temper my recommendation for advancement.

Most breakthrough discoveries, from learning how to start fires to putting a man on the moon, to developing I-phones, started with the same human condition: We are curious creatures born with the impulse to seek new information and solve problems. As we grow and mature, people line up to stifle this curiosity, however, fearing it will cause harm and compromise efficiency. The lucky ones among us also have people like Dr. Pearce who challenge us to develop our curiosity.

Building on the work of others, George Mason and Patrick McKnight created a five-dimensional model of curiosity. The first dimension, *deprivation sensitivity*, causes us to recognize a gap in our knowledge. Filling it offers relief. This type of curiosity doesn't necessarily feel *good*, but it causes us to feel better once we have a solution to a problem. For instance, a trip to the emergency room will give answers to the question about whether a person has had a heart attack. Both a "yes" or "no" answer will satisfy our curiosity.

The second dimension, *joyous exploration*, causes us to be consumed with wonder about the fascinating features of the world. This exploration produces a pleasurable state and joie de vivre among those curious enough to pursue answers.

The third dimension, *social curiosity*, encourages us to talk, listen, and observe others to learn what they are thinking and doing. Since we are inherently social animals, we find communication the most effective and efficient way to gain information that will allow us to determine whether someone is friend or foe. Some may even snoop, eavesdrop, or gossip to do so.

The fourth dimension, *stress tolerance*, relates to our willingness to accept and even harness the anxiety associated with novelty. People who lack stress tolerance see information gaps, experience wonder, and have an interest in others, but they don't tend to satisfy their curiosity by stepping forward and exploring.

The fifth dimension, *thrill seeking*, goes beyond tolerating stress to embracing a willingness to take physical, social, and financial risks to acquire varied, complex, and intense experiences. For people with this capacity, the anxiety of confronting novelty is something to be amplified, not reduced.[2]

In various ways, curiosity has the power to improve our lives. Empathic curiosity allows people to listen thoughtfully and see problems or decisions from another's perspective, not to criticize or judge, but to understand. Asking questions promotes more meaningful connections and more creative outcomes. When we carefully listen to the answers we seek, we build better relationships faster, fuel employee engagement, and reduce conflict.

Many leaders run their companies as if they fear curiosity will lead to a costly mess—and sometimes it does. More often, however, curiosity improves risk-taking because it reduces our susceptibility to stereotypes and to confirmation bias. It fosters collaboration and fortifies organizational resilience by prompting creative problem-solving in the face of uncertainty and pressure. In short, curiosity is the catalyst that brings job satisfaction, motivation, innovation, and high performance. When leaders can resist the temptation to erect barriers to curiosity, they boost both morale and performance.

Even though they might understand this concept, those with a fixed mindset can't afford to be curious. They seek confirmation bias—evidence that supports their beliefs and assures them they weren't wrong, even if they were. They don't generate alternatives because they don't believe they need any. Those who want to embrace and model a Disruptive Mindset do better. They convey their appreciation for curious employees:

- Reward creative failures. Most leaders eagerly reward success, but few have the guts to recognize the value of effort and experimentation, even when it fails.
- Understand that curious people learn quickly and bore easily, so they encourage continuous growth and learning.
- Don't try to trick the curious with empty titles. Give them ever-challenging work and real authority to make a difference.
- Make organizations places where the curious choose to work and allow stars to become magnets for other top performers.
- Don't saddle them with autocratic leadership or ignore them with a laissez-faire approach. Instead, give direction in the form of democratic guidance, not an absence of direction.
- Don't micromanage. If you try to micromanage a curious person just a little, you will lose that person.

I have spent my career selecting "A" players during the pre-employment and succession planning processes and then coaching them for promotion. They embody the aptitude, behaviors, and attitude of stars. Sometimes they lack experience, but when I detect curiosity, I know they will learn so quickly that gaining requisite experience won't stand in their way. Albert Einstein once said, "I have no special talents. I am only passionately curious." He got that half right. He had many special cognitive talents, but without his curiosity, perhaps none of us would even know his name.

COGNITIVE ILLUSIONS

In the nineteenth century, physicist and physician Hermann Helmholtz introduced the concept of *unconscious inferences*. We remember him for his "mathematics of the eye," which included theories of visual perceptions, space, and color. He helped us understand how we gain knowledge of the world through our conscious and unconscious perceptions.

We know how optical illusions occur. Almost daily someone posts something on Facebook that encourages readers to find the hidden number, icon, or message. When I taught the chapter on perception in psychology courses, nearly every textbook included the classic examples of the young woman/old woman or the picture of the vase that also included two faces. These examples pointed out how our perceptions influence our behavior and how our behavior influences our perceptions. But not all illusions are visual.

Understanding *cognitive* illusions offers more complexity. A cognitive illusion occurs when our mind relates the situation we're observing to something in our subconscious. In so doing, the image sparks our *subconscious* mind and brings a relatable perception into the *conscious* one, allowing us to use our assumptions about the world to create conclusions about what we see in front of us. Rather than merely *physically* seeing an object, therefore, we *mentally* create ideas about it.

Cognitive illusions can be more stubborn than visual illusions. Even when we recognize intellectually that we're experiencing an illusion, we don't always react logically. Our brain continuously tries to relate whatever information we already have with whatever we observe in the world around us. Sometimes we even make up stuff!

All this conspires against us when we face a risk-taking decision. We can't automatically turn off our illusions, so errors of intuition prove difficult to prevent. We can't always avoid our biases because we have no clue we harbor them. While continuous vigilance might improve our decision-making, constantly questioning our own thinking would be both tedious and impractical. We can learn to recognize quickly situations in which we and those around us are likely to make mistakes and try harder to avoid the mistakes when we face a high-stakes decision, but that often won't be enough. Daniel Kahneman, in *Thinking, Fast and Slow*, offers these recommendations for improving decisions:

1. Recognize when you're in a cognitive minefield. (Our intuitive thinking is prone to overconfidence.)
2. Slow down.
3. Ask for reinforcement.[3]

Unfortunately, we are least likely to apply this sensible approach when we sense the clock ticking or the pressure mounting. The voice of reason can be much fainter than the loud and clear voice of erroneous intuition. More doubt is the last thing we want when we face a risk, which makes the third recommendation the most important. We identify minefields much more easily when we observe others wandering into them than we do when we meander into them ourselves. Observers are less cognitively busy and more open to information than actors.

"Reinforcements," or those who haven't been part of the original decision-making process can prove invaluable because they can disturb the cognitive *illusion of unanimity* that occurs when the absence of obvious dissent leads others to conclude that the others concur. This can then lead to *collective rationalization*, the process through which people invent justification for their actions, causing them to feel they are acting in the best interest of a team. A "safety in numbers" mentality develops that can lead to excessive risk-taking when the group feels accountable to no one. The risk-taking that led to the Challenger disaster illustrates how cognitive illusions can lead to a tragic outcome.

On January 28, 1986, the Space Shuttle Challenger blasted off at an unprecedented low air temperature, breaking apart 73 seconds into flight, killing all 7 crew members aboard. The day before the disaster, executives at NASA had argued about whether the combination of low temperature and O-ring failure would be a problem. The evidence they considered was inconclusive, but more complete data would have pointed to the need to delay the launch.

The scientists at NASA and Morton Thiokol, therefore, felt the pressure of their bosses and the media to find a way to stick to the original schedule. Because the group discouraged dissenters, an illusion of unanimity surfaced, and the collective rationalization that allowed the decision-makers to limit their analysis led to their favoring a particular outcome—to launch on time.

Due to an extraordinary record of success of space flights, decision-makers developed an illusion of invulnerability, based on a mentality of overconfidence. After all, NASA had not lost an astronaut since the flash fire in the capsule of Apollo 1 in 1967. After that time, NASA had a string of 55 successful missions, including putting a man on the moon. Both NASA scientists and the American people began to believe the decision makers could do no wrong.

The Challenger tragedy illustrates that when you're in the throes of cognitive illusions, you can't always see or understand what's happening. A Disruptive Mindset, one that takes prudent not reckless risks, depends on leaders structuring a systematic approach for evaluating alternatives. Impartial leaders refrain from expressing a point of view until they have painstakingly listened to the perceptions of others. They assign *devil's advocates*, invite outside experts to examine information further, and set a *second-chance meeting* that helps decision makers avoid feeling "under the gun" by agreeing they will make no final decision during the first meeting.

Time and distance from the information allows people to avoid impulsiveness and quick-fix methodology. But it does more. When people can step away from their cognitive illusions and admit they are being influenced by them, they give themselves a chance to carefully evaluate the truly important aspects of the decision.

INTERESTING BUT IRRELEVANT FACTS

Several years ago, George, the vice president of a large publicly traded manufacturing company, hired me to help him formulate the strategy for his division. I had evaluated George as part of the succession plan, so I knew he possessed impressive cognitive skills. He learned fast, thought strategically, and knew how to make sense of the numbers. He did not, however, think dispassionately. Too often George allowed his emotions to distract him from the tough decisions he needed to make.

When I do strategy work, I use a proprietary process that helps clients think through the mission of the business, set objectives, and generally take today's risks to ensure tomorrow's results—the disruptive decisions they can't afford to get wrong. I strive to understand the company, culture, people, marketplace, and industry. Only then can I help them leverage opportunities and mitigate challenges. What I don't do is allow myself and others to get distracted by interesting but irrelevant facts. But George had other ideas.

I always encourage my clients to start strategy work with the leadership, *and only the leadership team.* George wanted to take a different approach and invite his direct reports and *their* direct reports—moving the number of people in the meeting from 5 to 20. Despite all our prework and best efforts, the strategy meeting quickly turned to a massive data dump with every camp weighing in, offering insight, and introducing interesting but irrelevant facts. The word "kerfuffle" springs to mind, but more objectionable terms would also apply.

No one asked the strategic questions: "So what?" and "Why?" and too many asked the tactical "How?" questions. Because so few people knew how to get to the core of complicated problems, zero in on the critical few, and put aside the trivial many, tactics took top billing, and strategy stayed undercover. George's fear that he would miss a detail caused him to chase ideas down rabbit holes from which they did not emerge, squandering the group's energy, time, and resources. I managed to turn the meeting in the direction we needed to go but not without considerable gnashing of teeth and lost opportunity.

In the debrief, George, who was more than a little proud of himself, wanted to hear my observations about how well he had handled the meeting. (He considered it a great success that he was able to hear so many facts in one day.) I suggested that he had heard many interesting things but not enough important ones.

He didn't seem to understand, so I pointed out that he should never have been drawn into a discussion about how they will hire a dumpster. In fact, I explained, no vice president should ever use the word "dumpster" in a meeting because doing so implies the conversation has gone far into the weeds, or, in this case, garbage. The problem? George didn't see it. Even after spending the day with 20 people in his chain of command, George still didn't know what pivotal decisions his team needed him to make, what calculated risks they should take, or what changes they needed to make to drive the business. In short, he had big data but not big judgment.

We had heard the "Voice of the Customer" report, read the survey results, and considered the interview findings. George heard it all, right up until the moment his eyes glossed over—indicating data overload. His consciousness in high gear, George tried to make sense of *everything* he had heard. George had scored at the 97th percentile on the critical thinking assessment, so I knew he understood how to prioritize and think strategically, but he lacked a *willingness* to do so. Instead, his fear of criticism that he'd overlook a detail caused him to be distracted by interesting but irrelevant facts. Ironically, this same fear of criticism also caused him to render his superior analytical reasoning skills irrelevant. As things turned out, George fared no better than those who would have scored much lower on the cognitive assessments. He didn't set a winning strategy for his team; his area began to lose money; and George eventually lost his job.

George's story has an unhappy ending because he had cognitive talents he refused to use. That stood in the way of him developing the expertise that would have shaped an enviable career for him and more success for the company he served. To better understand the nature of expertise, I offer four critical constructs: intelligence, talent, knowledge, and consistency of performance.

Although the ranking of these might differ, depending on the nature of the business, the most crucial forecaster of executive success is brainpower, or the specific cognitive abilities that equip us to make decisions and solve problems. When I assess leaders for selection or succession, I consider intelligence in three ways: critical thinking skills, learning ability, and quantitative abilities. Of these, *critical thinking* is the most important and the least understood.

Dispassionate scrutiny, strategic focus, and a global perspective form the foundation of critical thinking. These abilities equip a person to anticipate future consequences, get to the core of complicated issues, and immediately formulate solutions for never-before-seen problems. You can evaluate a person's critical thinking based on their track record of decision-making and the ability to do these:

- Separate strategy from tactics, the "what" from the "how"
- Overcome obstacles
- Create order during chaos
- See patterns, make logical connections, and anticipate consequences
- Multi-task
- Think on their feet

- Prioritize seemingly conflicting goals
- Paint credible pictures of possibilities and likelihoods
- Respond favorably to unexpected and unpleasant changes
- Serve as a source of advice and wisdom

Most people can learn to follow a protocol or set of procedures. Give them a checklist, and they can execute the plan. They know how to run fast, but sometimes they don't know which race to enter. Often these individuals are valuable employees, maybe even top performers. But they won't be stars without advanced cognitive skills.

General learning ability is the second most important aspect of leadership intelligence. When leaders acquire new information quickly, they don't lose valuable time moving through the pipeline. They evaluate new situations, learn about their people, learn about products and processes, and then immediately act on this knowledge. When this happens, the organization responds by moving the new leader's idea to action.

Reading ability, vocabulary, and fundamental math skills form the foundation of learning ability. Often, but not always, educational success serves as an accurate predictor of future learning success. People who learn how to learn early in their lives usually pick up speed throughout their lives. Certainly, ongoing learning teaches people about their own learning styles, so they become more proficient at acquiring new information and skills.

Although important to success at the top levels of most organizations, not every turn in the leadership pipeline requires quantitative abilities. Knowing what the numbers mean and using them to make sophisticated business decisions equips an individual to make budget or profit-and-loss assessments. Superior development of these skills allows a person to evaluate the nuances of mergers, acquisitions, and risk-taking ventures as they analyze strategy.

Numerical problem-solving, critical thinking, and proficient learning define the basics of business acumen. George excelled in all three of these areas, but that wasn't enough. George could not put aside true, often interesting, irrelevant information, so he never developed what it took to disrupt in constructive, productive, profitable ways. Had he been able to focus his attention and that of others on the truly critical aspects of running that manufacturing company, the story would have had a better—not just different—ending.

CONCLUSION

A neuron is an electrically excitable cell that communicates with other cells via connections called synapses. Synapses involve aggregation and unification of these neurons, which in turn form neural networks in our brains. That's how the *brain* works, but it doesn't adequately explain how we develop our minds or our mindset.

George Bernard Shaw said, "Progress is impossible without change, and those who cannot change their minds cannot change anything." A Disruptive Mindset is more about *action* than mere understanding. It involves changing one's mind and influencing the minds of others. Having a Disruptive Mindset allows a leader to deal with strategies and see changes, not as threats but as opportunities to make decisions to take dramatic actions that improve productivity and profits.

Mapping human neurons onto a computer, should that ever happen, won't give rise to consciousness in the computer. Neurons provide the material for human consciousness but cannot create it. That requires a rational mindset, proving that consciousness is more than an emergent property of electricity in the brain. Psychologist Carl Jung once said, "Thinking is difficult. That's why most people judge." Every company could improve with better discernment, but every organization that aspires to disrupt will have to think more too.

NOTES

1 Lyngar, S. (2010). *The Art of Choosing.* Pittsburg, PA: Twelve.
2 Kashan, T., Disabato, D., Goodman, F., and Naughton, C. (2018). "The Five Dimensions of Curiosity." *Harvard Business Review.* September–October.
3 Kahneman, D. (2011). *Thinking, Fast and Slow.* New York, NY: Farrar, Straus and Giroux.

6

Where You Going with That
Can of Gas?

A few years ago, while conducting 360 interviews for a construction leader, I asked one of his direct reports what he liked best about working for Kirk. He answered, "He understands what I'm feeling even when I don't." I hadn't ever heard that feedback before, so I asked him how he knew that. He said:

> Well, when he sees me storming out of here ready to rip someone's head off, he shouts, "Where you going with that can of gas?" His question always stops me, but it makes me laugh too. Once I tell Kirk what the problem is, he can usually calm me down and prevent me from saying something stupid that I'll regret later.

Kirk didn't know it, but he was advocating some sage advice: "Get your mind right before you open your mouth."

Why do some people trust their instincts, push forward, and win, while others stumble to wrong conclusions and then steadfastly defend their bad decisions? Why do some people rush to make bad decisions while others take their time and *then* make bad decisions? Whether thinking quickly or slowly, we rely on our emotions to help us make decisions. Then we open our mouths to let others know what that decision is. Most people would benefit from adding another step to the sequence, one that checks that they are advocating the *right* decision, not just the one they feel passionate about. Some theorists have said that to improve risk-taking, we need more emotional intelligence (EQ), but what does that really mean? It means we need to be more aware and empathic, in control, courageous, and decisive.

THE ART AND SCIENCE OF SELF-AWARENESS

In his book *Emotional Intelligence*, Daniel Goleman asserted that there are widespread exceptions to the rule that intelligence quotient (IQ) predicts success. At best, he contends, IQ contributes about 20% to the factors that determine life success, which leaves 80% to other forces. He also offered that we have "two minds"—the rational one and the emotional one—that work together to shape our destinies.

Don't believe it. We have one mind, one that often does not integrate cognition and emotion effectively, but still just one mind. Career success relies heavily on cognitive abilities, and general happiness related to "figuring things out" depends on the analytical reasoning skills to solve problems, especially emotionally laden ones, that have never happened before. Those who can't dispassionately evaluate solutions doom themselves to either bad decisions or reliance on others who *can* make good ones. Goleman and I disagree on the percentages, but we do agree on one thing: To our collective peril, we have ignored and misunderstood for too long the impact the role emotions play in decision-making.

Emotion is a major research growth area in neuroscience and psychology today, but that wasn't always so. In the 1960s, a search of psychological journals would have uncovered about 100 projects related to cutting-edge research about emotions. Emotion titles grew exponentially since then. In 2020, a Google search of "emotional research" cited more than 300,000 hits. Emotion has happened, but understanding its role in developing a Disruptive Mindset has not.

In his work on emotional intelligence, Travis Bradberry asserted that as a species, we are more self-aware. My experience tells a different story. He based his findings on 500,000 people *evaluating their own self-awareness.* The authors of *Now Discover Your Strengths* also based their conclusions on self-reporting. A chasm has opened, revealing significant differences among how we see ourselves, how others see us, how things really are, and how we interact with the world outside of us. We don't often accept the alien idea that events of which we are not aware have primed our emotions—causing us to act upon unconscious undercurrents.

We call this priming phenomenon—ideas influencing actions—the *ideomotor effect.* Much as people in history have relied on sticks (divining rods) to help them find water, people now experience a psychological phenomenon wherein they experience emotions and make motions unconsciously. We now know that divining rods only moved due to accidental or involuntary movements of the user, but we don't always detect how primers in the world trigger our own emotional responses. Consequently, we haven't been introduced to all the strangers in us. Even though we don't know all of them all the time, we can exert more control over them when we know ourselves better.

What happened? What is all the research about? You'll find different definitions for the term "emotion" and little agreement among researchers and theorists. We shouldn't be surprised. Despite discussions and debates that date back to the earliest days of modern biology and psychology, we have developed little consensus about what emotion is and how it differs from other aspects of mind and behavior.

If we don't agree on a definition of emotion that allows us to say what emotion is and how emotion differs from other psychological states, how can we study emotion in animals or humans, and how can we make comparisons among species? Much of the work on emotions has been done on animals. Mental states have a certain "feeling" associated with them and others do not. We call the states humans associate with feelings "emotions," but we also use "emotion" and "feeling" interchangeably.

In English we have words like fear, anger, love, sadness, and jealousy for these feeling states. When scientists study emotions in humans they typically use these "feeling words" as guideposts to explore the terrain of emotion—responses that occur when an organism detects and responds to significant events while surviving and maintaining well-being. Although emotions, or feelings, underpin the significant events in our lives, there has been relatively little connection among theories of emotion and emerging theories of consciousness in cognitive science.

Traditionally, theorists have based their studies of human emotion on fear and our responses to it, and certainly fear eclipses most other emotions in times of change, even positive, welcomed change. Even though planned disruption does not equal discontinuity, it frequently feels as if it does. But emotions we've long ignored do as well. Self-awareness, empathy, self-regulation, and ambiguity tolerance all add up to a different way of being smart—a way of thinking about our emotional intelligence. Although shaped by childhood experiences, emotional intelligence can be nurtured and strengthened throughout adulthood, with immediate benefits to developing a Disruptive Mindset.

Self-awareness involves a mindfulness of one's own personality and individuality. It should not be confused with consciousness. While consciousness includes an awareness of one's environment, body, and lifestyle, self-awareness identifies that awareness. Self-awareness means we recognize a feeling *as it happens*, and we spot emotions in others.

While conducting her research of nearly 5,000 participants, Dr. Tasha Eurich found that even though most people *believe* they're self-aware, only 10–15% actually fit the criteria. Her research suggests, however, that when we see ourselves clearly, we are more confident, creative, and successful. We make sounder decisions, communicate more effectively, and build stronger relationships. That makes us better leaders who get more promotions, and the companies where we work enjoy higher profits. Eurich came to three conclusions about self-awareness:

1. There are two types of self-awareness. *Internal self-awareness* represents how clearly, we see our own values, aspirations, and thoughts and how these impact others. *External self-awareness* means understanding how other people view us.
2. Experience and power hinder self-awareness. People do not always learn from experience, but seeing ourselves as highly experienced can keep us from seeking disconfirming evidence and questioning our assumptions.
3. Introspection doesn't always improve self-awareness. In fact, people who introspect are less self-aware than others. The problem with introspection isn't that it is ineffective; it's that most people do it incorrectly because we simply don't have access to many of our unconscious thoughts and feelings. They frequently remain trapped outside our conscious awareness, so we tend to invent answers that *feel* true but often aren't.[1]

Most people feel as though they know themselves well, but if they could know themselves a *little* better, they'd get a big payoff. Knowing who we are *and* how others see us forms the foundation for high performance, smart choices, and risk-taking. Self-awareness is a surprisingly developable skill. When we better understand ourselves *and* get others to tell us the truth about how we come across, we remove emotional blind spots that disguise the confidence we need to innovate.

SOCIAL AWARENESS STRATEGIES

Psychologists assure us that if you can "name it, you can tame it." Empathy builds on self-awareness: the more open we are to our own emotions, the more skilled we will be at reading the feelings of others—and the more in control we remain of ourselves and situations. When people *can't* identify their own emotions and don't understand why they feel the way they do, they can't comprehend what anyone else feels. When people experience this lack of self-awareness, we consider them emotionally tone deaf—unable to hear the notes and chords of the conversation. In more severe situations, we might deem them alexithymics.

The term *alexithymia* comes from Greek and literally means having no words for emotions. It is not a psychiatric diagnosis. Rather, it describes a personal trait characterized by the inability to identify and describe emotions experienced by one's self or others. People who experience alexithymia are marked by dysfunction in emotional awareness, social attachment, and interpersonal relationships. The failure to register *others'* emotions does several things. It prevents us from fostering trust, conveying respect, and strengthening two-way communication.

It also robs us of power. When we concentrate on what others *think* and ignore what they *feel*, we metaphorically enter a discussion with one hand tied behind our backs. In these situations, we forget that while logic makes us think, emotions make us act.

Although not the same, the capacity to feel empathy, the ability to *read* nonverbal signals, and the ability to *send* congruent verbal and nonverbal messages contribute to communication effectiveness. Why? People frequently can't find the words to express their emotions, so they express them in nonword cues. But they don't always understand the messages they send, much less the messages they receive.

Several years ago, I worked with an executive named Dan, an extremely gifted and focused engineer. At first, I didn't think he would experience any limitations to his potential in his highly technical Fortune 500 Company. But then I noticed that Dan had trouble connecting with people, which resulted in him experiencing high turnover. Before meeting him in person, I had spoken to him over the phone and had been impressed with his verbal ability and responsiveness, so I couldn't imagine why he was having so much trouble. Then, I met Dan in person, and all questions were answered.

Dan's nonverbal communication—his body language—contradicted his verbal messages and interfered with his ability to establish a strong executive presence. He wore a constant frown and look of discontent. Even when he talked about something pleasant, the frown persisted. But facial expressions were only one of his nonverbal problems.

Rather than telling Dan about my observations, I *showed* him. We videotaped a mock discussion that he might have with one of his direct reports. When I played back the video, I turned down the volume and asked him to *hear* with his eyes. He watched himself scowl and glower for two full minutes.

I asked Dan to forget that he knew the nature of the discussion and to guess what the speaker had been doing. He said, "It looks as if I'm trying to explain quantum physics to an oyster," (a little engineering humor).

As Dan learned, nonverbal communication plays a powerful role in all communication situations. Research shows that when we experience a discrepancy between the words we *hear* and the nonverbal message we *see*, we will most often trust the authenticity of the body language.

More than half of message sending can be tied to body language. Once Dan understood how his nonverbal language compromised his best efforts to communicate effectively, he controlled it, but he didn't come to this realization on his own. People need feedback about how they present themselves because, like Dan, we evaluate our communication effectiveness based on our *intentions*, rather than on the receiver's reaction to the message.

Clearly, a link exists between empathy and nonverbal effectiveness, but what role does cognition play? Most of my clients have exceptionally high critical thinking skills, so to find the answer to my question, I pulled the charts of top-performing executives I've worked with over the past 15 years to compare their analytical reasoning and empathy scores. The average analytical reasoning score was at the 75th percentile, which is above average, and the empathy average was at the 55th percentile, which is dead average. To answer the question about how much social awareness is enough, it seems that an average amount will do.

To better understand our fears and the emotions behind them, let's start with the psychological theory William Schutz proposed in 1958. This theory of interpersonal behavior postulated we have three core needs throughout our lives: inclusion, control, and affection. We want to feel part of something bigger than we are, to feel in control of our destinies, and to love and be loved.

Belonging makes us feel more secure and less afraid. For generations, families fulfilled this need for *inclusion*, but now we look beyond our families to others who make us feel as though we belong.

For instance, in 2019, the St. Louis Blues won the Stanley Cup for the first time. It seemed every man, woman, and child in the greater St. Louis area wanted to feel included in that victory. Everywhere you went for months after the championship, you saw Blues shirts. The day after the game, you couldn't buy a St. Louis paper with the headline. In fact, my copy of the *St. Louis Post Dispatch* disappeared from my driveway before 7 a.m. that day. Even clerks at the grocery stores put aside their uniforms to wear Blues shirts. This trend lasted well into the summer when everyone started wearing Cardinals baseball shirts—also meant to show solidarity with another St. Louis team.

People align themselves with others to experience these feelings of inclusion. The need that drives a young man to join a street gang is the same basic need that drives other young men to join fraternities. Belonging gives a sense of mastery too.

Control allows us to feel in charge of our own destinies—to experience steering our own ships. When we lose the feeling of control, we feel helpless and hopeless, the two hallmarks of depression. When we don't feel in control, we suffer *psychological* distress, but we shouldn't underestimate the *physical* price we pay for that.

In addition to feeling inclusion and control, we want to surround ourselves with people we like who like us. The most successful leaders I know, the ones who take the most risks and demonstrate the most advanced Disruptive Mindsets, know the people in their lives love them. They aren't all married, but they have friends and family that they know support them. When people stop nurturing the important relationships in their lives, they find themselves feeling cut off, lonely, and distressed. COVID-19 taught us some important lessons about our need for affection. When well-intended nursing homes sought to protect their residents from the virus, they also inadvertently shielded them from the interactions they craved. Many homes reversed their policies when they saw the devastation the isolation had caused, realizing that residents were more at risk for complications from social isolation than they were from the virus.

Can we have too much social awareness? The simple answer is "no." There's no such thing as being too knowledgeable, but problems can occur when leaders are too thin-skinned, touchy, sensitive, or humble. Tough calls become nearly impossible for people who don't create clear boundaries. Organizations thrive under the leadership of confident, decisive, assertive leaders who realize they have a responsibility to make the tough calls—even the unpopular ones. Meek, self-accusing, obsequious leaders don't usually remain leaders very long simply because they fail to read the environment around them and then to have the discipline to regulate themselves.

HAPPY PEOPLE SELF-REGULATE

In 2011, we learned of Arnold Schwarzenegger's love child, and a week later news of France's Dominique Strauss-Kahn's alleged rape of a hotel maid dominated the headlines. Two weeks after former Congressman Anthony Weiner's second unfortunate foray in the media, San Diego Mayor Bob Filner resigned amid allegations of 17 inappropriate sexual encounters.

In 2010, after General Stanley McChrystal made inappropriate comments in an interview with *Rolling Stone* magazine, President Barack Obama announced that General David Petraeus would succeed McChrystal as the commander of U.S. Forces in Afghanistan. In 2011, President Obama nominated, and the Senate confirmed General David Petraeus as the new Director of the Central Intelligence Agency. His tenure in the position would prove short-lived after his affair with Paula Broadwell was discovered.

What do all these once highly regarded, once happy men have in common? They didn't self-regulate, or they did for a time but then they didn't. Unfortunately, we usually remember people for their lapses in judgment, not their previous exemplary records or their stories that had happy endings.

People who self-regulate effectively *act* in their long-term best interest—to be consistent with their deepest values. They understand that a violation of their deepest values causes them guilt, shame, anxiety, and unhappiness. Those who self-regulate successfully can calm themselves down when they're upset and cheer themselves up when they're down.

"Emotion" comes from the Latin word "mot," which literally means "to move." The ancients believed that emotions *moved* behavior; in modern times we say they motivate behavior. Emotions energize us to do things by sending chemical signals to the muscles and organs of the body; they prepare us for *action*. Therefore, we are often tempted to discuss self-regulation in terms of these emotions that move us to act. However, self-regulation is more attainable when we focus on *values* rather than *feelings*—when we evaluate feelings as signals about reality and as means of self-regulations rather than as ends in themselves. Indeed, self-regulation is difficult when focused on feelings, simply because focus too often amplifies, magnifies, and distorts them.

Unlike Malcolm Gladwell, the author of *Blink*, I believe most people should not think without thinking or react without regulation. A select few may discover more creative solutions while mentally driving without a regulator, but the vast majority should not try it. When we see a leader "shooting from the hip," we shouldn't infer that's what's happening.

Instead, we should realize that most people need to gather data carefully, engage others in the decision-making process, anticipate consequences, and outline worst-case scenarios before pulling the trigger—or leave shooting out of decision-making altogether. For some, the process that leads to good decisions happens rapidly and unconsciously. That doesn't mean it doesn't happen at all. *Unconscious* processes are still processes. But I do agree with German psychologist Erich Fromm who advised, "Creativity requires the courage to let go of certainties." What occurs, then, at the intersection of self-regulation and happiness?

When I work with executives, one of the things I determine is whether they should listen to their instincts. For some, instincts prove right more often than wrong. For others, the reverse holds true. Here are the questions I encourage people to ask about themselves and others. These allow for an examination of their values rather than an exploration of their emotions:

- Do I want to make this change because of the rewards it may bring or the excitement it will guarantee? (If the former, go for it; if the latter, wait.) Not all great discoveries are made by gut instinct, flashes of insight, or reflexes. Some require painstaking step-by-step systems and attention to detail.
- What does my track record tell me? Have I been happy when I've listened to my instincts? Too many people see logic as a painful

systematic method that leads to paralysis. Consequently, they rely heavily on their impulses. Instincts have an emotional element to them, so introduce logic into the equation. Look at results to tell you if your way is working.

- Do I miss opportunities because I too often err on the side of caution? When I work with individuals who answer "yes" to this question, I encourage them to keep a log of their major decisions. As soon as they *think* they know the answer, I ask them to write it down along with the time and date. Then, I ask them to take as long as necessary to get the right answer and to note that time. Usually, when they look back, they realize they had made the right call the first time, and they lost time and opportunities by waiting. The exercise builds confidence that they should trust themselves sooner and more often.

These three questions get to the core of whether people should listen to their intuition, but they do more. They provide data from which people can define the gauges of success—the measures of how they will *personally* influence outcomes. When they understand this concept, they determine whether they tend to react impulsively or systematically. When they steadfastly focus on *outcomes*, they consciously act instead of reacting.

To build confidence that the next decision will be correct, start with the right mindset—one characterized by logic, a dispassionate review of your experience, and appropriate risk-tolerance. Add in a sincere desire to learn, and openness to new ideas, and you'll cook up a recipe for success and better decisions.

Emotions guide behavior. When we don't accept this fact, we make mistakes. Most people don't spend enough time examining *why* they feel the way they do. Instead, they spend most of their time thinking about *how* they think.

Because most businesses value logical thinkers, they tend to hire them for the upper echelons of the organization. There's nothing wrong with that. But those who overlook their own emotions and fail to recognize and identify others' emotions deprive themselves of valuable information that would allow them to make more informed, accurate decisions.

Leaders who possess a Disruptive Mindset have an emotional yet positive response to new and different information. They ask, "What might I learn by considering this new opinion, insight, or evidence?" Counterintuitive though it may seem, many otherwise exceptional people harbor feelings of insecurity. While they excel in one arena of their lives and enjoy the feelings of confidence that come from those achievements, general self-regard and self-respect may wane.

My research indicates that the engine of self-doubt drives the *behaviors* that cause the problems for the virtuosos. Others often don't understand the emotions behind the behaviors, since all objective measures indicate the virtuoso should feel confident and secure, but observable evidence will contradict this conclusion. When I coach virtuosos who indicate these emotions might be the source of their problems, I look for the root cause but then give them feedback related to how the emotions manifest themselves in day-to-day functioning and leading. One, or a combination of several of four, behaviors usually explains the problem: succorance, abasement, sensitivity, or exaggerated empathy. When people can pinpoint the cause of their behaviors, they tend to overcome the hurdles in changing problematic behaviors.

Of the plethora of emotive reactions, I find worry and guilt to be the Disruptive Mindset killers. Worry is a feeble attempt to control the future, while guilt is an equally useless effort to rewrite the past. Neither works, and both distract us from the hard word of problem-solving and decision-making.

Feelings make us human, create meaning, and motivate behavior. But they are never the *only* important—and rarely the *most* important—part of mindset-creation. Focusing on feelings without regard to values is more likely to lead to addictions and compulsions than helpful behavior. Consistent self-regulation requires an emphasis on a person's deepest values, not feelings. Violation of values invariably leads to guilt, bad feelings, and cognitive dissonance, while fidelity to them eventually makes people feel more authentic, empowered to face the fire-breathing dragons in their lives.

FEAR TOLERANCE

A few years ago, my daughter faced her biggest fear. Her then five-year-old son Andrew came screaming up the stairs from the basement to announce that there was a snake in the house. Not believing him, she boldly trudged down the stairs, scolding her son with her confident, "There's no snake in the house" mantra, only to spot the copper head in the middle of the floor, scream, run up the stairs, turn off the light, and shut the door. Turn off the light?

I know what you're thinking: Snakes can see in the dark. I don't know if they can or not, but Sherry reacted with emotion, not logic. When I asked her about this, she calmly explained that in the 30 seconds it took her to size up the danger and give in to her flee response, she had decided that she would never *ever* go downstairs again, and the snake could have the basement while she and Andrew would live out their lives happily upstairs.

At that point, she could have asked, "*Why* am I so afraid of snakes?" and answered, "Because I learned to be afraid from my dear, sainted mother." Instead she asked, "*What* am I really afraid of?" The second answer informed her that she was afraid of getting bitten by a poisonous snake, which was unlikely since Andrew had told her he thought the snake was dead, and we don't have too many poisonous snakes where she lives. She opened the door, turned on the light, and took a broom downstairs because everyone knows poisonous snakes are powerless in the face of a broom. The snake *was* dead; she scooped it up and took it outside, thereby claiming the basement for Andrew. A grateful son confided, "Mommy, you are so brave." She had become a hero to her five-year-old son.

There's nothing unusual about people fearing snakes. Most of us do. But it's rare to find people brave enough to face their fears and even rarer to find leaders who will admit their fears are irrational. No matter how toxic they may be, CUSTOMERS AREN'T ALLOWED TO BITE!

No visit with a customer will result in a trip to the emergency room. However, too many act as if they're killing snakes every time they walk into this situation. And we telegraph this fear, which makes us look less than confident, which causes the potential customer to distrust our capabilities. We create our own downhill spiral, give ourselves a shove down the slope, and rob ourselves of the motivation to get back in the game after a disappointment.

So, what relationship exists among our basic needs and fear? When my clients encounter someone behaving badly, I encourage them to ask, "What is the person afraid of?" The answer will probably be an exaggerated fear of one of three things: rejection, criticism, or loss of control. Similarly, when we realize we have behaved in a way that does not reflect our values, we do well to ask ourselves what we fear.

Reframing helps us forget long-held assumptions and abandon conventional mindsets, but it does something else. It frees us to discard the fear-driven, deficiency, scarcity mentality that holds us captive. If we can spot the signs, however, we can decide to think about things differently—to think the opposite of what we've always thought.

These fear-driven behaviors indicate the value in thinking differently:

Fear Factors

- The inability to celebrate and deconstruct success, to understand not just *that* you've succeeded but to understand exactly *how* and *why* you did
- A constant need for perfection and more information, even about non-critical issues
- Concentrating on cutting expenses—layoffs, plant closings, and outsourcing—versus growth
- Tolerating mediocre performers because "we can't afford superstars"
- Viewing employees as necessary costs, not valued assets
- A reluctance to develop top performers because they may take their new skills to the competition or, worse yet, they may challenge someone's position in the company
- An inability or unwillingness to learn and bounce back from failures
- Lack of clarity about the future
- Indecision, analysis paralysis, and finger pointing
- Taking low margin work to avoid "leaving money on the table"
- Vacillating when an opportunity presents itself, causing a loss of momentum
- Investing little in improvement
- A tendency to gloss over conflict, even when you know you're right
- Feeling overwhelmed, not in control, low energy, no joy.

Advancements in technology—developments that were meant to placate fears—have actually created more problems. A surfeit of information has changed the way we think—and not always for the better. Even though we now better understand how this phenomenon has occurred, it has crept up on us for a long time.

On the other hand, when we silence the fears in our heads, we clear the way for more dispassionate, rational thinking. That allows us to shift from a scarcity mentality to one of fortitude, one that encourages us to disrupt our comfort for a greater good. A mindset shift leads to better calls, but it starts with replacing fear with fortitude.

Those who live in harmony with fear have a quest for self-actualization and a desire to realize the fulfillment of their talents and potentialities—not a goal to overcome the competition. They don't allow competitors, customers, or employees to draw the map of their life positions. Instead of reacting with fear, they *proactively* create the playing field. Once people understand their strengths and ways to leverage them, they enter the more-promising, more-profitable arena of *self-competition*. In other words, as fear of failure and outside forces disappears, the self-actualized want to create more happiness, satisfaction, and fulfillment than they already have.

They let originality, not imitation, lead them. Imitation demands no special set of skills. Anyone can emulate, duplicate, or replicate. Innovation and uniqueness, on the other hand, require the courage to go where no one has gone before, to explore the new frontier, to discover what *can* be, not just what has always been. *Unoriginality* not only doesn't provide the safety net we crave, it leads us to where we were, not to where we need to go.

The boldest leaders I've worked with haven't expressed much interest in following the pack. Instead, they want to set the course with original thinking, which often means thinking on their feet. The ability to get to the core of complex, unfamiliar problems, zero in on the critical few factors, and quickly formulate solutions separates leaders of successful organizations from the "also rans."

Rick, the president of a construction company, is one of these leaders. At age 40, Rick faced the most complicated problem of his professional life. His client made unrealistic demands, expected him and his company to absorb cost overruns, and showed no willingness to help complete the project within a firm deadline. Rick lost sleep the first few times he encountered these never-before-seen problems. He lost sleep because the consequences loomed large and real. He lost sleep until he figured out that he *always* figures things out, and he would figure them out the next time too.

When people have a track record for solving problems, as Rick did, they build confidence and optimism. They tolerate their fears because they believe they can and will know what to do the next time they face the dragon. They don't expect to slay the dragon *every* time, but they have the confidence that they will emerge victorious more often than not, and the good guys will eventually win.

I ran into Rick a few months ago in an airport as he was returning home from a vicious legal battle with this client that had started six years earlier when I coached him. I asked how things had gone, and he admitted not as well as he had hoped. But he said two other things that impressed me. First, he said he had solved problems as well as anyone could have, and second, he had determined he wouldn't let this problem define his career, even though he had devoted six years of his life to fighting this dragon. He didn't exactly slay it, but because he overcame his fear of it, he managed to wound it better than anyone else could have. Rick leveraged his amazing critical-thinking strengths to move beyond the disappointments. He also realized he needed to develop new skills.

Like Rick, most successful leaders understand that what got them *here* won't get them *there*, wherever the next "there" happens to be. Yet, overusing a strength to the point that it becomes a weakness has reached epidemic proportion. Leaders who have moved up the corporate ladder relied on their independence to help them achieve. But at the upper echelons of the organization, they discover that others expect and demand teamwork. They often feel as though someone changed the rules in the seventh inning of the game.

The hard-charging, self-reliant, win-at-all-cost mindset spurs a fear-driven manager to become a leader, but this same mindset can cripple that same person who aspires to reach an executive level. It's getting lonelier at the top, so leaders who seek to improve must continuously acquire knowledge, change behaviors, develop skills, and take risks. Sometimes these leaders need help, so they seek it from people who have the expertise to give it.

They eagerly request the input of trusted advisors while eschewing unsolicited feedback. Seeking advice and counsel takes a certain degree of courage; rejecting unsolicited feedback takes even more fortitude and self-awareness. People with a strong commitment to self-improvement often eagerly and misguidedly take what they can get in terms of advice, analysis, and assessment. They overlook the fact that, more often than not, the feedback says more about the need for the giver to *say* it than the receiver to *hear* it.

Over the years, self-proclaimed experts have approached me and my fellow professional-speaking colleagues right after we have left the stage to ask, "Can I give you some feedback?" For years I responded, "Of course." Now, I simply say, "No thank you." Putting aside the need to seem overly responsive or the desire to be universally liked requires fortitude; patiently allowing someone to abuse the moment does not.

Successful leaders ask for constructive feedback when they want it, but they also show a willingness to deconstruct success. Having coached hundreds of leaders for thousands of hours, however, I can tell you unequivocally most people want to talk about their weaknesses more than they do their successes. When I open a feedback session with, "Do you have any questions before we get started?" Nine times out of ten, the person answers, "Yes. Tell me about my weaknesses and suggest what I can do about them." My response stays the same:

> You aren't sitting here getting ready for promotion because of your weaknesses. I only work with high potentials, and you're on the road to pro-motion, so wouldn't it make better sense to spend our time talking about how to leverage your *strengths*?

This usually brings a look of stunned disbelief, which every coach relishes.

Quashing fear moves the needle on self-improvement and makes tough calls easier, but no one should confuse the absence of fear with fortitude. Grit, pluck, determination, and valor define fortitude—with a little auda-city thrown in to help people have the courage to act on their beliefs. Although attributed to many, most believe Winston Churchill pointed out, "Failure is seldom fatal, and success never final—it's courage that counts."

Understanding our own emotions is the first step, but if we're going to cause disruption in our own businesses, we can't stop there. We need to understand the emotions of our direct reports, peers, investors, and customers too. Most of all, we need to stop fearing both success and failure. As Truman Capote once said, "Failure is the condiment that gives success its flavor." If we never fail, we end up with bland lives. You can be assured of that because the certainties of today quickly become the fallacies of tomorrow. Fear can make us uneasy, but it shouldn't debilitate us.

THE UPSIDE OF UNEASE

In 1957, Leon Festinger introduced "cognitive dissonance," a research-based theory that posits that internal psychological consistency helps us function in the real world. Cognitive dissonance refers to a situation that involves conflicting attitudes, beliefs, or behaviors. The theory suggests that we have an inner drive to hold all our attitudes and behavior in harmony and avoid disharmony (or dissonance).

People who experience internal inconsistency tend to become emotionally uncomfortable and motivated to reduce the cognitive dissonance—to decrease discomfort and restore balance. They tend to make changes to justify the stressful behavior, either by adding new parts to the cognition causing the psychological dissonance or by avoiding circumstances and contradictory information likely to increase the magnitude of the cognitive dissonance. The more important the decision, the more dissonance we experience since, obviously, important decisions have more serious consequences than trivial decisions.

For example, when people smoke (behavior), and they know that smoking causes cancer (cognition), they find themselves in a state of cognitive dissonance. To restore balance, they must either discount the research about cancer-causing effects of smoking or quit smoking. Indeed, millions have quit smoking because of the cognitive dissonance they experienced when they learned of the harmful effects of smoking, but millions have not. They have chosen to live in a state of disharmony, which causes more stress, more dissonance, and more disease. When inconsistencies exist between attitudes or behaviors, something must change to eliminate the dissonance.

Feelings of powerlessness contribute to stress, but ironically, they reduce dissonance. When others mandate a course of action, we're off the hook. We may get angry, but we no longer feel the internal tug of war about what we should do. We quit maneuvering for a way to enjoy the advantages of the unchosen alternative while accepting the disadvantages of the chosen one, primarily because there is no good option for opening schools and businesses. There are just some options that don't seem quite as bad as others. That doesn't mean that we can't still work to reduce dissonance.

A way to reduce dissonance is to *increase* the attractiveness of the chosen alternative and to *decrease* the attractiveness of the rejected one. This is referred to as "spreading apart the alternatives." But what happens when we don't like either choice, but we have to make a decision? The same advice applies: Reduce discomfort by evaluating chosen options more favorably and evaluating unchosen options less favorably.

We can reduce dissonance in four ways:

1. Revoke the decision. (Just refuse to make it.)
2. Dwell on the benefits of the chosen alternative.
3. Stress the drawbacks of the unchosen option.
4. Reduce the importance of the decision.

Making decisions causes dissonance, especially if the chosen and unchosen alternatives have similar drawbacks. However, hundreds of experiments have demonstrated that after making a difficult decision, compared with an easy one, individuals change their attitudes to be more consistent with their decisions; individuals evaluate the chosen alternative more positively and the rejected alternative more negatively than they did before the decision.

In his 1971 classic, *The Farther Reaches of Human Nature*, Abraham Maslow introduced the word "resacralizing." He had to make up words like this because, in his opinion, the English language has no decent vocabulary for the virtues. Readers understood that desacrilizing, often a defense mechanism, involves removing the sacred status or significance from an idea or point of view, even mistrusting the possibility of values and virtues. Resacralizing doesn't *defend* the sacred; it demands the courage to rediscover value. Leaders who resacralize trust their own voices, take responsibility, and work hard to determine what's right, not just what's right now.

Leaders who engage in the hard work of living with unease and resacralizing move decisions ahead more quickly because they don't allow themselves to get distracted by that's-the-way-we've-always-done-things thinking. They overcome their fear of making a mistake, but when they do make one, they bounce back and live to decide another day.

My advice is to follow my dad's advice about making decisions: Learn everything you can about your options; control what you can control; make the decision; and then forget about it. Worry and guilt will only distract and terrorize you. The steps we must take to reduce cognitive dissonance can serve as a springboard that fuels better decisions, more confidence, and success—if we let it.

The upside of unease is we can learn to take the critical actions that allow a company to withstand an onslaught, whether that comes on the winds of war or the reptilian creep of a pandemic. When leaders understand their ambiguity tolerance, they embrace some of the fundamental responsibilities during turbulent times:

- Leverage strengths to survive the blow.
- Adapt quickly to the new reality.
- Position the organization to leverage new opportunities.
- Create an organization that can survive so it has a chance to thrive.

Einstein advised, "Imagination is more important than knowledge." Be clever and conscientious but never stop imagining. To do otherwise is to capitulate and to experience the emotional drain of decision fatigue. They may say you're a dreamer, but you won't be the only one. You'll surround yourself with other clever problem-solvers too.

CONCLUSION

Bertrand Russell advised, "The degree of one's emotion varies inversely with one's knowledge of the facts—the less you know the hotter you get." Russell understood that when we face new realities, don't deny them, and stay cool, we can focus on innovation, even when it involves risk. When we understand ourselves better and the environments in which we work and live, we can apply self-discipline, overcome fears, and tolerate ambiguity. We don't allow ourselves to get distracted by illusions and half-truths, no matter how appealing they seem.

As Sheik Ahmed Zaki Yamani once pointed out, the Stone Age, which lasted a little more than three million years, didn't end because we ran out of stones. Instead, modern-day archeologists have determined that it ended with the advent of metalworking. Like our prehistoric ancestors, we too face new realities and a time of transition from what we once understood, and often held dear, to what we must learn to live with and appreciate. When we understand our emotions and learn not to pour fuel on them, we take important steps in the direction of goodness.

NOTE

1 Eurich, T. (2017). *Insight: The Surprising Truth About How Others See Us, How We See Ourselves, and Why the Answers Matter More Than We Think*. New York, NY: Penguin Random House.

7

The Truth about What Motivates Us to Change Our Mindsets

In the early days of psychological research, when blackberries and apples were still just fruits, psychologists sought reasonable explanations for why humans behave the way we do. Theorists often overlapped and built on each other's ideas, but, just as frequently, they *disagreed*. We expect more from scientists! We want someone to develop a blood test or diagnostic scan that allows us to "have a look" at how much motivation a person has. We want to measure it, so we can control it. Alas, neither option exists.

Renowned Notre Dame football coach Lou Holtz observed, "Motivation is simple. You eliminate those who are not motivated." Sage advice for selecting football players and employees, but is it really that simple? Motivation moves us to action, but it does more. A kick will cause a dog to move, but we shouldn't infer the canine acted because of any kind of intrinsic motivation. Rather, the poor dog wanted to avoid further pain. Human motivation tends to be more complex. We don't limit ourselves to actions associated with reward and punishment. Instead, we have evolved natures and myriad social, cultural, religious, and family influences.

Yet we don't fully understand why people behave the way they do. Why do wide variations in behavior occur? I consistently and conscientiously strive to answer these questions when I help clients make high-stakes decisions about succession planning. I examine how once-motivated people can lose the desire to learn, change, and grow, but I'm most intrigued by those who never lose their drive and constantly strive to fuel it.

THE MOTIVATION MANIFESTO

In high-stakes situations, we see a gap between what science knows and what business leaders do. Science has carried out extensive experiments on mice, monkeys, and humans to reach conclusions about what makes us tick, but, when it comes to understanding motivation, we've barely scratched the surface.

We may agree that all mentally healthy people are motivated, even when they aren't motivated by the same things. But does that knowledge really help? Much of what we believe about motivation just isn't true, and most businesses haven't caught up to what *is* true. Many still operate on assumptions about human potential and individual performance that are obsolete, unexamined, and rooted more in folklore than in science.

In the face of mounting evidence that such measures usually don't work and often do harm, many leaders continue to pursue practices such as short-term incentive plans and pay-for-performance schemes. Worse, these practices have infiltrated our schools and youth athletic programs, where we ply our future leaders with trophies and pizza coupons to "incentivize" them to learn and develop. If this approach ever worked, and I suspect it did not, it no longer does.

Research demonstrates that giving people what I call "growth goals" helps them develop competence and acquire skills, which boosts motivation. Productivity objectives, on the other hand, can often have the opposite effect. When motivated by growth goals, we do better work and make better decisions. Most organizations know how to set performance objectives, but few recognize the value in setting growth goals. Leaders at Deloitte knew better.

In their 2019 Global Human Capital Trends report, Deloitte stated that people now rate the opportunity to learn among their top reasons for taking a job. Eighty-six percent of their respondents rated this issue as important, yet only 10% felt ready to address it. The numbers imply that people are worried about how technologies such as robotics and artificial intelligence could change jobs, and people recognize they should prepare for an unknown future.

Top performers have always been motivated to learn, but recent advancements have caused many to understand they also need to "reskill." Reskilling has become a growth imperative for organizations, many of which have seen positions go unfilled for months or years for lack of the right talent to fill them. The already motivated see the writing on the wall and want to prepare for it, but too few organizations have learned how to respond to this need to learn. Without it, however, those who aspire to develop a Disruptive Mindset don't stand a chance.

Humanistic psychologist Carl Rogers focused his work on what he considered an innate motivation to become our best selves. This drive for fulfillment enables people to enhance themselves, but it does more. Increasing awareness of true feelings causes the self-concept to become more congruent with the total experiences of the individual. Complete harmony—or as close as most people can get to complete harmony—within the person then allows full functioning or self-fulfillment. Rogers pointed out that the process of discovering the good life is not for the faint-hearted. It involves the stretching and growing of becoming more and more of one's potentialities. It requires the courage to be. It means launching oneself fully into the stream of life.

Rogers identified the "real self" as the "you" that, if all goes well, you'll become. But we don't always receive a great deal of support for developing our real selves. Instead, well-intended people try to help us become our "ideal" (meaning not real) selves. That's when incongruence sets in. Our ideal selves are always slightly out of our reach—a standard we cannot attain. This gap between the real self and the ideal self, the "I am" and the "I should" causes us to become demotivated.

Rogers recognized the need for positive regard from significant others in the formation of self-concept, personality, and motivation formation. He added that this positive regard is contagious. That is, only one person in the relationship needs to feel congruence for changes to occur in *other* people. I'm not sure that's true, but this is an empowering statement for leaders. If Rogers is right, leaders may possess more power or control than they might have previously perceived.

While many earlier researchers grappled with the roles innate characteristics and environmental conditions play in personality formation, Rogers saw a significant gap remaining. No earlier theorist had adequately emphasized the roles of *interpersonal relationships* and the individual's *frame of reference* in the person's development. Carl Rogers educated us about how we develop motivation, but Will Rogers explained that "Even if you are on the right track, you'll get run over if you just sit there." They're both right. We are all motivated but often by different things.

For example, my sister and I grew up in the same house, same culture, and same time in history. We have the same parents, wore the same clothes, and attended the same churches and schools. We look alike and share many of the same interests, yet we find different things motivating. We both have demanding jobs, hers as an ICU nurse manager and mine as a consultant. Our jobs differ, but our need to unwind at the end of the day is eerily similar—just not identical.

I enjoy doing crossword puzzles. As a former English teacher and avid reader, I enjoy language and solving puzzles that use words. Mary Pat, who earned a perfect score on the math section of the SAT, finds numbers relaxing, so she does Sudoku. I have often said that heaven and hell would differ for the Henman girls. Hell for me would involve sitting in a cold room by myself, forced to do math story problems for eternity. That describes heaven for Mary Pat.

We receive neither a reward nor a punishment for our hobbies, yet each evening will find us engaging in our recreational puzzle-solving. Why? What motivates us to pursue these activities on a regular basis, when psychologists have assured us we do things to seek reward or to avoid pain? Or, as Freud posited, for love, work, or the love of work? A third drive, or motivator, must make us do these kinds of things that don't pass conventional motivational litmus tests—a drive to accomplish and to receive the *emotional* rewards of a job well done.

In the 1940s, psychology professor Harry Harlow wanted answers. From his work with rhesus monkeys at the University of Wisconsin, he formulated the theory of a *third* drive. At the time Harlow started his work, theorists generally accepted that *two* main drives powered behavior—the biological drive that causes humans to eat, drink, and copulate, and the second drive to seek reward and avoid pain.

While the biological drive came from within, the second drive came from without—the rewards and punishments the environment delivered in response to certain behaviors. In other words, we are motivated to receive rewards like a paycheck and motivated to avoid pain, like not having enough money to pay our bills. But Harlow and his team stumbled upon something else—a drive that causes us to want to achieve.

To test his hypothesis, Harlow and his team devised a puzzle that required monkeys to do three things: pull out a vertical pin, undo a hook, and lift a hinged cover. They placed the puzzle in the cages of the monkeys to observe how they would react. Something unexpected happened. Even though solving the puzzle did not lead to a reward, and no punishment occurred if the monkeys didn't solve the puzzle, the primates kept at it, determined to figure out a solution.

No one taught the monkeys how to remove the pin, slide the hook, or open the cover. No biological need or reward/punishment explanation made sense. Harlow concluded we needed a new theory to explain this third drive: the drive to perform a task for the pleasure of figuring it out. My sister and I do our nightly puzzles for much the same reason the monkeys solved the puzzles: we enjoy it. Accomplishing a task has its own intrinsic reward—which leads to intrinsic motivation.

At first, Harlow thought the other two drives would subordinate this third new one. Of course, he theorized, if the researchers *also* rewarded the monkey with raisins, they would see even more motivation to solve the problem. Yet, when Harlow tested this idea, the monkeys made *more* errors and solved the puzzles in *less* time. The promise of an extrinsic reward actually interfered with intrinsic motivation. This body of research certainly flew in the face of conventional wisdom and encouraged psychologists to close down their "theoretical junkyard" to offer fresher, more accurate accounts of human behavior.[1]

Early science didn't help us understand motivation at work, largely because people with jobs tended to have their biological needs covered. Also, people with jobs had figured out how to seek rewards and avoid pain. Therefore, most businesses haven't caught up to newer insights about what motivates us, even though Harlow completed his work more than seven decades ago. Finally, we have realized we need a dynamic, integrated approach to understanding human motivation.

Even though expounding on possible reasons for human behavior has occurred for centuries, psychology is a relatively new science that emerged as an independent scientific discipline in Germany during the middle of the nineteenth century. Practitioners defined its task as the analysis of *consciousness* in the adult human being. Then, psychologists realized they should be paying attention to the *unconsciousness* too, the place where motivation lies.

We humans continuously and inevitably find ourselves in the grips of a conflict among opposing forces that Freud called the id, ego, and superego and that others called nature/nurture. I call the mindset that emerges from this battlefield the "Disruptive Mindset," and its origins don't matter. Awareness does.

HOW PYGMALION INFLUENCES MOTIVATION

From Greek mythology, we remember Pygmalion as an excellent sculptor who devoted himself to his art, which spared him no time to admire the beauty of women. In fact, legend informs us that Pygmalion shunned women, finding solace only in his craft. One day, Pygmalion carved a statue of a beautiful, graceful woman in the form he most desired. Enchanted by his own creation, he fell in love with his creation and called her Galatea.

On the day of a celebration to Aphrodite, Pygmalion prayed to the goddess, beseeching her to turn his ivory figurine into a real woman. Touched by his deep veneration, Aphrodite granted Pygmalion his wish and turned his perfect sculpture into a perfect woman. Their love blossomed, and the couple lived happily ever after.

Building on the myth, George Bernard Shaw wrote *Pygmalion*, a clever adaptation about Professor Henry Higgins, a linguistic expert who takes a bet that he can transform an awkward Cockney flower seller into a refined lady simply by polishing her manners and changing the way she speaks. Like his mythical counterpart, the professor also fell in love with his elegant handiwork, but unlike Galatea, Eliza Doolittle did not return his affection. As Eliza explained her situation,

> You see, really and truly, apart from the things anyone can pick, the difference between a lady and a flower girl is not how she behaves but how she's treated. I shall always be a flower girl to Professor Higgins because he always treats me as a flower girl and always will.

Robert Rosenthal and Lenore Jacobson later developed "The Pygmalion Effect" to explain how people in positions of power can influence the development and motivation of others. They began by studying children and their teachers' perceptions of them. They showed that if teachers were led to expect enhanced performance from children, then the children's performance improved, supporting their hypothesis that teachers can positively or negatively influence self-fulfilling prophecies.

In Rosenthal and Jacobson's study, students in a single California elementary school took a disguised IQ test at the beginning of the study, but the researchers did not disclose the scores to the teachers. Instead, they told the teachers that some of their students (about 20% of the school chosen at random) could be expected to be "intellectual bloomers" and identified the bloomers.

At the end of the study, all students again took the same IQ test used at the beginning. All six grades in both experimental and control groups showed a mean gain in IQ from before the test to after the test. However, first and second graders showed statistically significant gains favoring the experimental group of "intellectual bloomers." This led to the conclusion that teacher expectations, particularly for the youngest children, influence student achievement. Rosenthal and Jacobson received criticism of their work for both weak methodology and lack of replicability. That doesn't mean their conclusions weren't accurate, nor was their work the only one of its kind to engender disapproval.

The assassination of Martin Luther King Jr. in 1968 prompted educator Jane Elliott, a white schoolteacher in an all-white third-grade classroom, to create the now-famous "Blue Eyes/Brown Eyes Exercise." Elliott wanted her students to understand what discrimination felt like, so she split her students into two groups, based on eye color. She told the children that people with brown eyes were superior to those with blue eyes, for reasons she invented. Brown-eyed people, she told the students, are smarter, more civilized, and better than blue-eyed people. Therefore, she told them, these brown-eyed students should receive special privileges. She watched with horror at what she saw.

The students started to internalize and accept the characteristics they'd been arbitrarily assigned based on the color of their eyes, changing the behavior of both the brown-eyed students and the blue-eyed students. Further, the way the children *treated each other* changed markedly.

I first watched a video of the Elliott experiment when I studied diversity in graduate school in the 70s. She taped actual footage of the students and herself. I too watched in horror. Thirty years later, I saw the video again, this time at the request of a diversity consulting firm that wanted to work with me to develop diversity training programs for my clients.

Again, I watched in horror, but my reaction had changed with a more in-depth education in psychology. The second time, I was outraged by the things that disturbed me the first time I saw the video, but this time I was equally shocked that Elliott, a non-psychologist, had experimented on children to satisfy her own curiosity about how we develop prejudices. And I was more than a little incensed that this consulting firm that specializes in diversity and inclusion training saw nothing wrong with using this video to make a point with my clients. I severed that relationship.

Rosenthal, Jacobson, and Elliott all violated research protocols (children can't give informed consent) and ethics in their experiments, and all three invited criticism of their methodologies. But that doesn't mean their conclusions were wrong. IQ, self-fulfilling prophecies, prejudice, and motivation all respond to the influence of others. When others tell us, especially the youngest among us, things about ourselves, we frequently believe them. Sometimes that works in our favor, bringing out the best in us because we know someone whose opinion we trust has faith in us. We believe both athletic and business coaches who shout from the sidelines, "You've got this!" Unfortunately, we also believe the negative voices that get stuck in our heads that say, "You're not good enough." Many of my executive coaching clients tell me that the biggest benefit in working with me is that they build their self-confidence by hearing the "tape" of my voice in their heads.

Like Professor Higgins, most leaders unintentionally treat their subordinates in ways that lead to lower performance. However, if leaders set high expectations for disruptive decisions, innovation will follow. If leaders' expectations are low, innovation will follow that trajectory too. It seems an immutable law of physics exists in the business world that causes direct reports' performance to rise or fall to meet bosses' expectations. Similarly, if leaders expect disruptive innovation and reward both *effort* and results, they will get it. If they expect slight improvements to the status quo and reward stability, they will successfully achieve sameness.

Heretofore, neither theorists nor leaders themselves have understood the importance of setting disruptive expectations for individuals and groups. However, irrefutable evidence leads us to believe that direct reports, more often than not, appear to do what they believe they are expected to do. It all starts with leaders. What leaders believe about themselves and their own abilities to innovate subtly, and sometimes dramatically, influences what they believe about their direct reports, what they expect of them, and how they treat them. Savvy leaders understand that "dangling the carrot" just beyond the donkey's reach, once endorsed by motivational theorists, does not serve as an effective motivation device. It just makes for a very unhappy donkey and employees who make donkeys of themselves. Effective leaders understand that a leader's greatest challenge is to rectify the underdevelopment and underutilization of their direct reports' innovation potential.

As we strive to develop a Disruptive Mindset, our job is to silence all the negative voices in our heads that keep repeating critical messages and to turn up the volume of all those positive voices, confirming current and previous messages that assure we can become the best version of our "real," not ideal selves. Leaders can take a page from Pygmalion's book and do their part to sculpt a workforce that embraces innovation. That may not always work, but the least they can do is to create a culture where the best people can do their best work.

HOW DOES THE ENVIRONMENT AFFECT MOTIVATION?

How many people have ever tried to get a teen-aged boy to unload the dishwasher? This same young man, who voluntarily suits up in 100-degree August heat to attend two-a-day football practices, has to be held at gunpoint to do simple household chores. He's motivated by a grueling physical workout but not by mundane duties, which lends credence to the observation that all people are motivated—just not by the same things.

In *Guns, Germs, and Steel*, Jared Diamond asked "Why did wealth and power become distributed as they now are, rather than in some other way? Why did human development proceed at such different rates on different continents?" These questions led him to conclude that history followed different courses for different peoples because of differences among peoples' environment, not because of biological differences among the peoples themselves.

For instance, Diamond detected a key role of competition in spurring innovation. As he noted, Germans make wonderful beer, probably the best in the world. Yet the productivity of the German beer industry is only 43% that of the U.S. beer industry. Meanwhile, the German metalworking and steel industries are equal in productivity to their American counterparts. If the Germans can organize industries well, why can't they do so when it comes to beer?

The German beer industry suffers from small-scale production. Tiny beer companies dot the German landscape, but they are shielded from competition with one another because each German brewery has virtually a local monopoly, and they are also shielded from competition with imports. The U.S. has 67 major beer breweries, producing 23 billion liters of beer a year—31 times more beer than Germany's 1,000 breweries combined. In Germany, there is no competition, just a thousand local monopolies.[2] The environment in Germany lends itself to making good beer but not to disrupting the status quo. If the goal of German beer makers were to surpass beer production in the U.S., they would have to change their laws and radically change the way they do business. I suspect they are interested in doing neither.

Industry leaders don't have to manufacture competition. It exists. But too often I've seen leaders create competition within their four walls—conflict among competing goals. When leaders do this, they intentionally or inadvertently pit employees against each other. Sometimes this creates a contest to see who can win a race for more sales, but more often it interferes with collaboration and compromises creativity and innovation.

About ten years ago I saw a dramatic example of this. While working with a financial management company on their succession plan, I detected the leadership team was comprised of exceptional solo performers who completely lacked teamwork. I pointed this out to the CEO and asked if he saw this as a problem. He said that 90% of the time it was okay. I asked him what would happen if they worked together the other 10% of the time. He said it would increase the shared bonus pool several million dollars! So even though each person would have earned enough extra money to buy a new luxury every year, the team resisted cohesion.

When they disrupted their mindsets and realized how much money each man was leaving on the table, they committed to a new way of doing business—a way that demanded innovation from this group who clung tenaciously to the status quo. Even in 2020, in the throes of a pandemic, this firm has significantly increased its assets and bonus pool. For years I have reported the research indicating that money is not a motivator, but that conclusion doesn't always apply to money managers. Their work revolves around making money for their clients, so it makes sense that they would feel motivated to benefit from their own knowledge of how to make more money. It wasn't easy, and it took a long time, but eventually, this leadership team altered their mindsets.

For almost a century people have studied *why* people work, but a major breakthrough happened in the 1980s when professors Edward Deci and Richard Ryan distinguished six main reasons why people work: play, purpose, potential, emotional pressure, economic pressure, and inertia. The first three motives tend to increase performance, while the latter three hurt it. Leaders who create an innovative culture maximize the good motives while minimizing the bad ones.

Play motivates us to "play with ideas," to learn, to experiment, and to explore challenging problems. "Play" explains why my sister and I do puzzles to relax. We enjoy it. *Purpose* suggests we value the work's impact. It gives us meaning, and the outcome fuels our identity. *Potential* benefits that identity and enhances our potential. For example, project managers might find their current jobs motivating because they aspire to be project directors. These three motivate us and help us improve performance and innovation.

Indirect motives, however, tend to reduce both. People experience *emotional pressure* as fear, peer pressure, and shame. When we do something to avoid disappointing ourselves or others, we're acting on emotional pressure. These internal and external punishments act independently of the work itself. We might be tempted to think of emotional pressure as a demotivator, but traditional psychological theorists agree that we feel motivated to avoid pain.

Economic pressure occurs when an external force makes us work. We work to gain a reward (a paycheck) and to avoid a punishment (financial ruin). In these cases, motivation remains separate from both the work itself *and* the person's identity. This often leads to *inertia*, the tendency for motive to be so far removed from the work and the people's identity that they can't identify why they're working. Paradoxical though it may seem, inertia describes a motive because people continue to do the work, they just can't explain why they do it because it lacks play, purpose, and potential.[3]

One of the most striking myths about motivation involves the inaccurate assumption that if we can "read" people and situations, we know ourselves too. And, if we know ourselves well, we will understand what motivates us. Ian, a senior sales leader at a large company, certainly thought so. He prided himself on his ability to size up a sales situation quickly and to close the sale faster than anyone could. Ian took more interest in *why* people did what they did than in *what* they actually did. He enjoyed the complexities evident in human personality, motivation, and behavior. Not always practical in his approach, he succeeded nonetheless in keeping his pipeline humming. He closed more deals than anyone else at the company and quickly rose to the top where the company expected him to oversee the success of other salespeople. Instead of his psychological insights serving him well in his new role as sales leader, they served as a pebble in his psychic shoe. He felt the constant nagging feeling he had missed something, but he couldn't identify it, even though up until *then* he could zero in on *exactly* what caused sales to soar or tank.

In our work together, I assured Ian he wasn't losing his touch. He still understood how and why sales happen, and he had a fairly firm grasp on what motivated his sales team. He just didn't understand what made *him* tick. He lacked self-awareness.

He required more. He needed to understand better how to harness his passion for selling and derive the same satisfaction from leading *others* to more impressive sales goals than he felt with his own accomplishments. He didn't understand how changes to his role had changed the environment from one where he did his best work to one where he felt his motivation wane. He failed to discern patterns in *his* behavior, so he also overlooked the effect he had on others.

Ian dispelled an important myth—the one that says, "Motivation comes from within, so there's little a leader or other outsider can do to influence it." Not so! Most people consider themselves self-aware, just as most people consider themselves good drivers, but judging from the number of auto accidents every year and the number of failed business ventures, we must challenge *those* myths too. Most people most of the time need a trusted advisor to help them identify their sources of motivation and to discover how to make more satisfying decisions. Only with feedback do we see our behavior objectively, so only then can we take steps to behave in ways that reveal our motivation.

DOES A BURNING PLATFORM REALLY MOTIVATE?

In July 1988, a disastrous explosion and fire occurred on the Piper Alpha oil-drilling platform in the North Sea off the coast of Scotland. One hundred and sixty-six crew members and two rescuers lost their lives in the worst catastrophe in the history of North Sea oil exportation. Andy Mochan, however, survived.

Andy woke to the sound of the explosion and alarms. Badly injured, he escaped to the platform edge—facing the decision whether to remain on the burning platform and ensure his death or to jump into the freezing water where he knew he could survive for only 20 minutes. Andy jumped

15 stories from the platform to the water. When asked why he took that potentially fatal leap, he replied, "It was either jump or fry." He chose *possible* death over *certain* death. Was Andy Mochan motivated to jump? You bet. He jumped because he felt he had no choice.

We remember the burning platform story, not because of the horrifying incident, but because in 2011, Nokia CEO Stephen Elop wrote his roughly 1,300-word memo to shake up the phone company's leadership. The memo outlined the perilous situation facing the company that was once the world's leading mobile phone company. The memo likened the situation of Nokia, in the smartphone market, to a person standing on a burning oil platform. "Platform" referred to the name given to operating systems such as Symbian, Apple iOS, and Google Android.

We now use the term "burning platform" to describe a situation where people feel forced to act by dint of the alternative being worse. Arguably, a burning platform will motivate people to act in the moment, but can most people stay motivated once the crisis has abated?

Rosabeth Moss Kanter, former editor of the *Harvard Business Review*, pointed out that burning platforms do serve as powerful drivers of strategic change when:

- We face a real and immediate crisis.
- We perceive a limited number of difficult and challenging choices.
- Each of the choices is irreversible.
- Each choice has a high risk of failure.

Burning platforms do motivate, at least in the short run. Once a crisis becomes obvious, burning platforms motivate people to act. That's the good news. The challenge of achieving a transformation, however, becomes more daunting, and time is not your friend. You'll have precious little time to explore alternatives. Stakeholders and shareholders will not tolerate the mistakes that they would have tolerated in ordinary times—missteps that can prove fatal.

Leaders who try to motivate by creating a burning platform want to scare their employees into changing. They paint such a pessimistic picture of the current state of things that employees can't help but jump into the freezing sea, metaphorically speaking. Without doubt, if you need quick and specific action, fear can motivate. In a crisis, emotional pressure will move people to action.

But as Deci and Ryan taught us, emotional pressure over time compromises productivity and morale. When we attempt to live in a constant state of crisis, then anger, resentment, guilt, and worry overpower creativity, flexibility, and innovation—and all these interfere with the development of a Disruptive Mindset. When leaders motivate by painting optimistic but credible pictures of the future, they show others purpose and potential—especially in high-stakes environments.

Motivation moves us to action, but it does more. To stimulate continuous improvement and productivity, people with Disruptive Mindsets question the status quo. They press for new and innovative ideas as opposed to just maintaining the "this is the way we've always done things around here" mindset. They enjoy experimenting with new approaches and pioneering novel ideas. They become champions of and agents for change.

They don't advocate change for its own sake, however. Innovation can only happen if you have innovative thinkers making decisions. *Nothing* changes otherwise. When you hire smart people and create an environment that rewards innovation, you can improve just about anything. (Notice, I didn't say "change." Change for the sake of change is really annoying.)

A crisis that won't go away can cause the once-motivated people to join forces with the never-motivated—as much as inertia can be described as a force. In a threatening environment, they then quit making tough calls because they don't see the point. What good does it do? Feeling like victims trapped in a mental hospital, they often flee the asylum, taking their expensive training, experience, and expertise to the competition.

ACCOMPLISHMENTS GIVE US PLEASURE

In a recent conversation, my friend Craig informed me that the company he worked for would probably call him back in January 2021 when contracts resumed after the pandemic. However, they had mentioned he would be working for a reduced salary. Craig said that would probably also mean they got a less motivated, less productive employee in him. I told him he's wrong. Craig has had careers as a fighter pilot, airline pilot, and his current one as an aviation instructor. He attained the rank of Brigadier General in the Air National Guard and flew as a captain on wide-body aircraft. This man is not capable of mediocre performance, no matter what the salary. I told him so.

He might imagine he won't be as motivated if he thinks he's not being compensated fairly but having known this man for more than 35 years, I assured him he had two choices. Retire or work as hard as he always had. There is no third choice that would make him feel good about himself. Why? He needs to achieve.

Craig offers a good example of *Self-Determination Theory* (SDT) in action. This theory of human motivation and personality addresses people's inherent growth tendencies and innate psychological needs—the motivation behind choices people make without external influence and interference. SDT focuses on the degree to which an individual's behavior is self-motivated and self-determined.

In the 1970s, research on SDT evolved from the growing understanding of the dominant role *intrinsic* motivation played in an individual's behavior. Intrinsic motivation refers to the initiation of an activity for its own sake because a person finds it interesting and satisfying, as opposed to doing an activity to obtain an external (extrinsic) goal. However, SDT would not be widely accepted as a sound empirical theory until the mid-1980s. Previously mentioned researchers Deci and Ryan later expanded on the early work differentiating between intrinsic and extrinsic motivation and proposed three main intrinsic, universal, and innate needs involved in self-determination: competence, autonomy, and relatedness. The study of conditions that *facilitate* versus *undermine* intrinsic motivation is an important first step in understanding sources of both alienation and liberation of the positive aspects of human nature.

Competence involves the inherent tendency to grow and develop—to control the outcome of an activity and experience mastery of that task. The rhesus monkeys experienced control when they solved the puzzle. I reap the rewards when I complete a crossword puzzle (especially a *New York Times* one), and my sister feels it when she masters another Sudoku. Craig felt it when he received his wings, and he experiences it each time he certifies a new student pilot. My children and grandchildren sense it when they play video games. People want to feel competent to operate within their important life contexts.

Curiosity fuels competence, creating an upward spiral of striving, achieving, and energy. It wanes, however, when challenges are too difficult, negative feedback is pervasive, or feelings of mastery are diminished by critical and social comparisons. Competence can't fly solo, however. It will not enhance intrinsic motivation unless accompanied by a sense of autonomy.

Humans share a need for *autonomy*. We are inherently proactive with our potential and mastering our inner forces like drives and emotions. Autonomy centers around actions involving a sense of volition and self-endorsement rather than on people's self-concept, identities, or self-evaluation. Autonomy requires self-regulation and self-sufficiency, but it compels more. It demands independence and the reduction of inner conflicts. When we can become agents of our own lives and act in harmony with our integrated (real) selves, we feel motivated to develop competency in new areas and to overcome the challenges we'll face in doing so.

Relatedness describes the universal need to be connected to others and experience caring for them. We want to feel we belong—to experience significance among others. Abraham Maslow called this need "belonging," while William Schultz called it "inclusion." Most personality and motivational theorists agree that optimal development and actions are inherent in humans, but they do not happen automatically. To actualize our inherent potential we need nurturing from the social environment.[4]

When we satisfy these needs, we're motivated, productive, and happy. When we or others thwart them, our motivation, productivity, and happiness plummet. Much of the research guided by SDT has also examined environmental factors that *hinder* or *undermine* self-motivation, social functioning, and personal well-being—the deleterious effects that thwart our three basic psychological needs. Thus, SDT is concerned not only with the specific nature of positive developmental tendencies, but it also examines social environments that are antagonistic toward these tendencies.

SDT is an important part of the new thinking about what makes us behave as we do. Others who have influenced this movement include Abraham Maslow, William Schutz, Martin Seligman, Carl Rogers, Carol Dweck, Dan Gilbert, Frederick Herzog, and Hans Rosling, among others. These players in the positive psychology movement, which has shifted the focus away from the study of malady and dysfunction and toward well-being, has helped us learn more about what it takes to develop a mindset that will serve us as we face change and risk. It offers hope that we can play major roles in *causing* positive disruption instead of just responding to external positive and negative disruptions.

CONCLUSION

Researchers, theorists, and management consultants have long asked the perennial question, "How do you install a generator in an employee?" The simple answer is you don't. You can certainly create an environment where the motivated can flourish, but no one can create achievement drive where none exists. Lee Iacocca was right when he said, "Motivation is everything. You can do the work of two people, but you can't be two people. Instead, you have to inspire the next guy down the line and get him to inspire his people."

Unfortunately, most of us believe the best way to motivate ourselves and others is with external rewards. That's a mistake. We need to realize the secret to productivity and success lies in the deeply human need to take control of our lives, to grow, and to feel connected to those we love or admire. Then, we put ourselves in a position to heed the advice of Joan Baez, "Action is the antidote to despair."

NOTES

1 Harlow, H., Harlow, M., and Meyer, D. (1950). "Learning Motivated by a Manipulation Drive." *Journal of Experimental Psychology*. 40.
2 Diamond, J. (1997). *Guns, Germs, and Steel*. New York, NY: W.W. Norton & Company, Inc. P. 435.
3 Deci, E. and Ryan, R. (2018). *Self-Determination Theory*. New York, NY: The Guilford Press.
4 Ibid.

8

Resilience Is an Offensive Weapon

Psychologically healthy people want power and authority over their futures. When we perceive control in our lives, we feel optimistic and secure. When we don't, we feel persecuted. We start to feel undermined, overwhelmed, and immobilized—powerless. People who find themselves in this mindset seldom take risks. They see any uncertainty as fraught with peril, which causes them to throw possibilities and opportunities out as assuredly as they discard threats.

However, those with a Disruptive Mindset do better. Because they start with resilience and hardiness, they feel confident they will bounce back from adversity, should it raise its ugly head. Most resilience theories and research, including my own original research on the Vietnam Prisoners of War (VPOWs), offer plausible, practical explanations about what resilience is and how it improves our lives. Almost all the theories overlap in what I call *The Four Building Blocks of Resilience*™: Resilient people have searched for and found meaning; they share a pragmatic view of reality; they extemporize as they follow their life's path; and through it all, they take their problems seriously but themselves lightly.

WHAT IS RESILIENCE?

Ordinarily, the definition of a term states what it *is* rather than what it *is not*. However, trying to find agreement among researchers about the definition of "resilience" is akin to asking poets to share one opinion about the word "love."

Psychologists began to research resilience in earnest when Norman Garmezy arrived at the University of Minnesota in 1961. Professor Garmezy wanted to identify children who would be more resilient in the face of stress versus those who would develop more adjustment problems. He concluded that resilience played a greater role in mental health than anyone had previously suspected. Experts widely credit this marriage of developmental and clinical approaches with the birth of the field of *developmental psychopathology*.

Building on this work, other researchers began to explore the "protean self," a concept that takes its name from the Greek god Proteus who could change shapes to protect himself. These researchers found specific protean characteristics and determined that the mutable self emerges from confusion—from the widespread feeling that we are losing our psychological moorings. The emergence of the changed self allows for a more resilient self—one with a resilient mindset. While the protean self may experience pain and trauma, it is able to transmute that trauma into various expressions of insight, compassion, and innovation.

Later researchers defined resilience as a combination of *externally* observable adaptive actions and *internally* held hardiness about one's own life. That is, resilience is tied to the ability to adapt and adopt. By 1982, researchers at the University of Chicago had concluded that hardiness—commitment, control, and challenge—functions to decrease the effects of stressful life events. This constellation of personality characteristics serves as a resistance resource in the face of stressful life events.

The commitment disposition involves a tendency to involve oneself in—rather than experience alienation from—whatever one encounters. Committed people, therefore, have a generalized sense of purpose that allows them to identify with and find meaningful the events, things, and persons of their environment. They invest themselves in action, not passivity or avoidance. They commit to people, ideologies, dogmas, and missions; and in return, they receive peace of mind and comfort.

Hardy people also feel and act as if they have control over their environments. They feel influential rather than helpless. Control enhances stress resistance perceptually by creating a kind of self-fulfilling prophecy. In other words, when we take control of our reactions to changes in our lives, we increase the likelihood that we will experience events as a natural outgrowth of our actions and, therefore, not as foreign, unexpected, and overwhelming occurrences. Control leads us to act in ways that transform events into something consistent with our ongoing life blueprint—making them less jarring and more welcome aspects of our plan.

The disposition to embrace challenges comes from the belief that change, rather than stability, is normal. When people anticipate change and see it as an interesting incentive to grow, they avoid feeling threatened by the loss of steadiness that constancy offers. An appreciation of challenge also mitigates the stressfulness of events by coloring them as *stimulating* rather than *intimidating*, even when the change involves readjustment. Challenge also allows the integration and effective appraisal of even exceedingly incongruent events.

In his work, *Mysterium Coniunctionis* (The Mysterious, Mystical Union), psychologist Carl Jung explained the path of the hero and offered some insights about how the true hero faces and overcomes challenges:

> In myths the hero is the one who conquers the dragon, not the one who is devoured by it. And yet both have to deal with the same dragon. Also, he is no hero who never met the dragon, or who, if he saw it, declared afterwards that he saw nothing. Equally, only one who has risked the fight with the dragon and is not overcome by it wins the hoard, the "treasure hard to attain." He alone has a genuine claim to self-confidence, for he has faced the dark ground of his self and thereby has gained himself.... He has arrived at an inner certainty which makes him capable of self-reliance, and attained what the alchemists called the unio mentalis (the unity of mind).

Notice some of the lessons Jung offers. First, there is no heroism in not ever having challenges to conquer. On the contrary, we admire most those who have fought the fight and won, not the ones who have never had a fight to fight. Second, Jung points out that the same dragon will devour some people but will be conquered by others. The dragon, or the adversity, remains the same; however, the person opposing the dragon differs. When we develop the necessary coping skills to fight adversity, we maximize the opportunities for emerging victorious, not scarred.

In 1980, the *Diagnostic and Statistical Manual of Mental Disorders* (DSM-111) introduced the term "Posttraumatic Stress Disorder" (PTSD) to describe the psychiatric disorder that can occur in people who have experienced a traumatic event such as a natural disaster, a serious accident, a terrorist act, combat, rape, or other violent personal assault. We had previously called PTSD by many names, such as "shell shock" during World

War I and "combat fatigue" after World War II and Vietnam. But PTSD does not just happen to combat veterans. It can occur in all people of any ethnicity, nationality or culture, and age. PTSD affects approximately 3.5% of U.S. adults, and an estimated one in 11 people will be diagnosed with PTSD in their lifetime. Women are twice as likely as men to have PTSD.

People with PTSD have intense, disturbing thoughts and feelings related to their experience that last long after the traumatic event has ended. They may relive the event through flashbacks or nightmares; they may feel sadness, fear, or anger; and they may feel detached or estranged from other people. What they don't feel is safe, connected, or in control.

In a corporate setting, a Disruptive Mindset that allows people to take strategic risks is not just about responding to a one-time crisis—although that helps. It's about continuously anticipating and adjusting to deep, secular trends that can permanently impair the earning power of a core business. It's more about having the capacity to change *before* the case for change becomes desperately obvious rather than avoiding the crippling effects of PTSD *after* the event.

In my 1998 doctoral dissertation, *The Vietnam Prisoner of War Experience: Links Between Communication and Resilience*, I used the words *hardiness* and *resilience* synonymously and defined them as "the capacity to cope with and to survive traumatic conditions and to recover from adversity, as measured by the absence of a psychiatric diagnosis." Researchers don't all agree on the definition of resilience, and indeed I'm not even using the definition I used previously; but we do agree about what resilience *is not*. It is not sickness, pessimism, or failure to adapt.

For this discussion, therefore, I define resilience as "the capacity to cope with and recover from adversity." It implies an ability to "bounce back." But that leads to questions like "Why can some people bounce back from adversity while others languish? Why can some leaders help those around them find the path through the crisis when others can't?" It all starts with a search for meaning.

THE PURPOSE-DRIVEN LIFE

The ability to find meaning in difficult times forms the foundation of resilience. Those who can find purpose in adversity are less likely to throw up their hands asking, "Why me?" Those who fail to find meaning in hardship paint a picture of victimization for themselves and start to feel like the prey in a B-rated movie. Sometimes people stay in a victim's frame of mind long after a loss or disappointment. They doubt their capacity to make their lives happen according to their own aspirations, so they wait to be rescued or blessed by good fortune. Those who have the capacity to bounce back fare better.

Anthropologist Gregory Bateson asserted that to communicate and to establish meaning within oneself and between individuals forms the core of our humanness. That is, consciousness and purpose have been characteristics of people for at least a million years, and from these we develop the wisdom to recognize what we need to do to save ourselves from danger. As self-corrective systems, we can absorb disconcerting information and frame it like a pearl so that it doesn't make a nuisance of itself. Therefore, creating a purpose-driven life happens when we consciously or unconsciously admit some stimuli and reject others. But when we're forced to admit disturbing truths, we also have the ability to figure out how to cope with them.

People use language to share experiences—good, bad, and indifferent— which then leads us to find meaning in a situation that ostensibly seems meaningless. "Meaning" is the concept that links the symbol-making process with a continuous function of humans tantamount to eating and sleeping. Therefore, resilient people create concepts about their suffering to conceive some sort of meaning for themselves and others.

The literature on resilience suggests that our beliefs influence resilient behaviors and feeling a part of "something bigger" contributes to our ability to recover. People devoted to a higher cause are more likely to build normal lives after their release from the prisons of disappointment.

Some theorists contend that the most vital ingredient of resilience is faith. Sometimes this faith undergirds a specific religion or secular beliefs, but the faith is also anchored in our relationships to one another. This sort of foundation serves as a unifying pattern that organizes our deepest convictions about ourselves and our place in the world as it creates our truths. Faith, therefore, is the *unseen order* the individual perceives from within.

Coping resources encompass the ability to change the meaning of a bad situation, helping a person develop a "things will work out as well as can reasonably be expected" attitude. For several reasons, avoiding apathy is perhaps the most complicated of the constructs of resilience. Finding meaning in a situation that seems devoid of it is an *intrapersonal* undertaking, but the creation of meaning among individuals involves *interpersonal* behavior. Both are key to avoiding an unhealthy apathetic reaction.

Most studies on resilience show that people who turn toward others for support tend to reverse negative consequences of an initially destructive experience. Also, reversing the perception of *victim* to that of *rescuer* gives survivors a sense of mastery or control. In other words, taking action to help others and avoiding apathy fuel social support networks, which ultimately contribute to resilience. Communication allows people to use symbols, metaphors, and rhetoric to create reality within themselves and between each other.

No discussion about leading a purpose-driven life would be complete without a nod to Victor Frankl, a Holocaust survivor and the author of *Man's Search for Meaning*. As Frankl pointed out, "Everything can be taken away from a man but one thing: the last of the human freedoms—to choose one's attitude in a given set of circumstances, to choose one's own way."

Frankl believed that striving to find a meaning in one's life is the primary motivational force in man. Other research supports that conclusion. However, Frankl also wrote

> On the average, only those prisoners could keep alive who, after years of trekking from camp to camp, had lost all scruples in their fight for existence; they were prepared to use every means, honest, and otherwise, even brutal...in order to save themselves. We who have come back. We know: The best of us did not return.[1]

This would imply that resilience is neither ethical nor unethical—neither good nor bad. It is merely the skill and capacity to be hardy under extreme conditions. My research on the VPOWs suggests a different conclusion: Through the creation of social support and interdependency, the fiercely independent VPOWs learned to rely on their own powers to create meaning and to draw a sense of mastery from one another. Ordinary men were able to do extraordinary things because their system of finding purpose acted as a type of anchor in humanity. Because they were cemented in a strong social structure, they had a buffer against alienation and apathy. Their dedication to one another was a powerful civilizing force that discouraged any antisocial slip into a kind of jungle mentality. This allowed them to return with honor, boasting the fewest incidences of PTSD of any other group in captivity. As VPOW Jim Mulligan put it,

> For out of the miseries had come strength; out of the suffering, compassion; out of hate, love. If nothing else, I would come home a better man than when I entered there. Life would be more meaningful in every aspect from now on.[2]

Our values and beliefs aid us in finding meaning in our own lives and in sharing our truths with others. We think of most of the world's religions as unified systems of beliefs—creeds that govern behavior that one generation chooses to pass on to the next. Most world religions were founded on the principle that those who shared espoused beliefs would augment the meaning in their lives if they were to share them with others, too.

In an organization, espoused values reflect those perceptions that leaders consider "correct." Over time, employees of a given organization learn that certain values work to reduce uncertainty in critical areas of the organization's functioning. As the espoused values continue to work, they gradually transform into an articulated set of beliefs, norms, and operational rules of behavior. Eventually these values become embodied in an ideology or organizational philosophy that serves as a guide for dealing with ambiguity or difficult events. Then we call this "culture."

When a solution to a problem works repeatedly, people start to take it for granted. The hypothesis, supported only by a hunch, comes gradually to be treated as a reality. Basic assumptions become so taken-for-granted that no one challenges them. Therefore, they influence behavior, even when people don't mention them.

Looking within oneself, finding the purpose, and then having faith that there is meaning helps to ameliorate the unspeakable. Furthermore, being able to rely on others for support augments the coping that occurs within the individual, especially if this support occurs within the context of a well-defined system. VPOW Jerry Coffee wrote:

> Faith was really the key to my survival all those years. Faith in myself to simply pursue my duty to the best of my ability and ultimately return home with honor. Faith in my fellow man, starting with all of you here, knowing you would be looking out for my family, and faith in my comrades in those

various cells...Faith in my country, its institutions and our national purpose and cause....And, of course, faith *in my God—truly, as all of you know, the foundation of it all.*[3]

Gregory Bateson's ideas about people not only *possessing* but *being* self-corrective systems are particularly cogent to this discussion. As he pointed out, part of creating meaning involves using mechanisms to edit that which stands in the way of creating meaning. By rewriting that which they find disturbing, people can rid themselves of information that would make a pest of itself and put their energies toward making sense of their lives. Selective perception can work for the individual and does not have to lead to pathological denial or apathy. Rather, it can lead to pragmatism.

PRAGMATISM

In his 2001 bestseller, Jim Collins introduced a powerful psychological duality that he named the "Stockdale Paradox." According to Collins, on the one hand, the companies he studied stoically accepted the brutal facts of reality. On the other hand, they maintained an unwavering faith in the endgame and a commitment to prevail as a great company despite the brutal facts.

The Stockdale Paradox refers to admiral Jim Stockdale, the second-highest ranking officer among the VPOWs, second only to Robbie Risner (Collins refers to Stockdale as the highest-ranking officer, but Risner outranked him by two weeks). Stockdale, who endured nearly eight years of imprisonment and extremely harsh treatment confided in Collins,

> This is a very important lesson. You must never confuse faith that you will prevail in the end—which you can never afford to lose—with the discipline to confront the most brutal facts of your current reality, whatever they might be.[4]

The fascination with pragmatism began as a philosophical movement in the U.S. in 1870. This tradition included those who claimed that an ideology is true if its meaning can be found in the practical consequences of accepting it. Pragmatists, therefore, contend that most philosophical topics—such as the nature of knowledge, language, concepts, meaning, belief, and science—are all best viewed in terms of their practical uses and successes. They consider words and thoughts as tools for prediction, problem-solving, and action; and they reject the idea that the function of thought is to describe, represent, or mirror reality.

My research of the VPOWs suggests several pragmatic conclusions: Resilience involves a collective effort; it's contagious; and it is comprised of universal ingredients, with competition being among them. Outwitting the guards and strategizing to avoid torture or to gain desired outcomes served as a primary method of coping. While they didn't compete with each other for scarce resources, the VPOWs did fill their hours with physical and mental contests that also brought them a feeling of accomplishment.

The competition in question differs from a definition we might automatically apply. The men cooperated and coached each other to rise to new levels of performance, even when this level of achievement meant the coach would lose a first-place position. Push-up and sit-up competitions were among the most common. Sometimes the contest existed within the individual to increase his own best number, but other times the men in one cell competed with those in another cell block.

Mental competitions often involved bets, involving the use of collateral one would not normally use. For instance, one participant said he heard another remark, "Well, I now own your wife and kids. What else are you willing to bet?" One participant reported that he left captivity owing another man a case of Korbel Champagne. Upon repatriation, he priced a case and sent a check to cover his losses. It was the game of strength or wits held the appeal, not the ante.

The pragmatism the VPOWs developed had more to do with practicality and less to do with ideology. For instance, the Code of Conduct developed after the Korean War would *ideally* have guided the behaviors of the VPOWs, but as they quickly learned, a theoretical, untested code had little relevance to their survival. Admiral Stockdale, therefore, ordered the men to ignore the directive that they withstand torture. Instead, he embraced a more realistic, sensible decision that advised those in his chain of command to avoid the permanent psychological and physical ramifications of torture. Stockdale assumed he would be court-martialed for issuing the order. Instead, he has been lauded as one of the strongest leaders in the annals of military history. To be pragmatic, therefore, is to be practical, realistic, rational, sensible, reasonable, and sane, even when others insist on idealism.

How does pragmatism affect businesses? In short, every business is successful—and pragmatic—until it's not, but too few leaders anticipate the "not." These leaders, the ones who choose to hunker down and wait for the shock to dissipate, don't anticipate disruption, so they have no willingness to cause it and few tools for managing it. But to thrive in turbulent times, organization must become as effective at disruption and strategy decay as they are at producing products and services.

In their *Harvard Business Review* article, Hamel and Valikangas noted that leaders must

> face up to the inevitability of strategy decay. On occasion, Bill Gates has been heard to remark that Microsoft is always two or three years away from failure…Change will render irrelevant at least some of what Microsoft is doing today—and it will do so sooner rather than later.

And while it's easy to admit that nothing lasts forever, it remains more difficult to admit that a dearly beloved strategy has gone from ripe to rotten.[5] Even the best strategies can lose their distinctiveness, get replaced by better strategies, become exhausted as markets become saturated, and invite evisceration when an unknown player joins the game or when a competitor makes an unforeseen winning move.

Resilient leaders share an unblinking attitude about the parts of reality that matter to survival. They embrace optimism and value its role in helping them stay hopeful, but they also develop both preventative and contingent plans to augment it.

Not only do we see rapid change in the world, leaders can no longer anticipate the shockingly turbulent times that lie ahead. Who predicted the devastating effects of COVID-19? Leaders didn't see it coming, nor did they foresee how quickly the shock waves would go through their business or industry. No longer will successful leaders rely on "what is" or even "that's the way we've always done it" investments. Instead, they will develop the psychological muscle to start asking "What can we be?"

PSYCHOLOGICAL MUSCLE

Nature or nurture? Do people come into the world armed with genes to fight the pathologies that would prevent resilience? Many theories about resilience stressed the role of genetics in helping develop hardiness. Often, they argued, we see resilient children born to resilient parents, which implied, at least tacitly, that we inherit a predisposition to bounce back from adversity. But wouldn't the fact that biological parents raised the children also make a strong case for "nurture"?

More recent studies have shown that resilience can be learned. For example, George Vaillant, the director of the Study of Adult Development at Harvard Medical School, observed that within various groups he studied during a 60-year period, some people became markedly more resilient over their lifetimes. They developed what I call "psychological muscle."

In his book *Aging Well*, Vaillant asked what makes for successful maturation— what are the factors that separate the "happy-well" from the "sad-sick" in later life? Six factors measured at age 50 predicted those who would be in the "happy-well" group at age 80: a stable marriage, a mature adaptive style, no smoking, little use of alcohol, regular exercise, and maintenance of normal weight.

Building on the work of previous scholars, Vaillant studied 268 members of the classes of 1941 through 1944 for an in-depth, lifelong study of "normal" adult development. At age 50, 106 of the men had five or six of these factors working in their favor, and at 80, half of this group were among the "happy-well." Only eight fell into the "sad-sick" category, the bottom quarter of life outcomes. In contrast, of 66 men who had only one to three factors at age 50, not even one was rated "happy-well" at 80. In addition, men with three or fewer factors, though still in good physical health at 50, were three times as likely to be dead 30 years later as those with four or more factors.

As Vaillant's study confirms, our defenses are always better when we are not hungry, angry, lonely, tired, or drunk. Feeling safe, secure, and "held" allows us to develop the psychological muscle that will sustain us through hard times. Also, although it is not easy to change our defenses by ourselves, fortune favors a prepared mind. We can start by admiring how other skillful people cope and by pondering how we might have used self-defeating mechanisms when things went wrong for us.[6]

When we take care of ourselves in good times, we build the psychological muscle, or what Vaillant calls "mature adaptive style," that will steer us in

152 • *Resilience Is an Offensive Weapon*

the right direction when things turn sour. When we learn to improvise, we rely on our psychological muscle memory.

Unlike octopuses, we don't have brains in our limbs, so we can't really "remember" anything in our arms and legs. But once we learn to ride a bike, we never forget. It sure *feels* as if our bodies "remember" how to do it. Most people refer to this phenomenon when they talk about "muscle memory." Psychological muscle memory works in much the same way.

Some psychologists have called psychological muscle *bricolage*, a French loanword that means the process of improvisation or tinkering. Those who can engage in bricolage have an ability to extemporize a solution to a problem they have never encountered before. In the world of music, we say that those who can simultaneously compare, perform, and sing on the spur of the moment without any preparation "improvise." When people make do with the tools and materials on hand—usually to fill an unforeseen and immediate need—we think of them improvising, too.

The bricoleurs among us tinker and play with ideas—constantly painting credible pictures of possibilities. After assessing thousands of executives in pre-employment and promotion situations, I have found this ability most related to advanced critical thinking skills, and in previous writing I have called it "strategic thinking abilities."

People with this kind of psychological muscle constantly keep a global perspective, continually asking "what?" before "how?" They don't let obstacles stop them and can create order during chaos. They see patterns and trends before anyone else does, and they can think on their feet. They also quickly and adeptly set priorities, setting aside the trivial many while zeroing in on the critical few. Surprises don't derail these bricoleurs because their psychological muscle memory triggers their best instincts.

Resilient organizations are replete with these bricoleurs who know what race to get into. These companies don't *survive* setbacks; they *thrive* in the newly minted reality, whatever it is.

HUMOR AND LIGHT-HEARTEDNESS

The fourth building block of resilience is the ability to find humor in life's dramas—a willingness to take ourselves lightly even as we face grim realities. In his 1977 book, *Adaptation to Life*, George Vaillant maintained that adaptability is a primary component of resilience, and a sense of humor is a trait of effective adaptation. His later works confirm the importance of mature adaptive style, with humor being an element of that style. When facing adversity or unwelcome change, humor helps humans become skillful psychological scavengers.

Change and adversity, often mentioned in the same breath, frequently tempt us to see unexpected, unwanted change as a hardship, a pervasive loss of control. The ancient Chinese, however, saw things differently. They indicated their understanding of change by constructing a two-part pictogram that appears to imply contradictory thought. The bottom part by itself includes the character that means "opportunity." The top character alone means "danger." To the Chinese, change includes part danger and part opportunity, a wise and insightful understanding.

Danger and opportunity often arrive at the party simultaneously and play roles in the lives of people who are experiencing some sort of transition. Too often, however, we resist change or become immobilized by it because we fear our altered circumstances will bring more danger than opportunity.

Researchers have given us some useful information for understanding and predicting people's reactions to change and for identifying some of the coping behaviors that help us adjust to the stress that upheaval causes in our lives. Humor is a much-needed addition to this coping repertoire.

Change, or transition, can be defined as *the process of moving from here to there*. Change involves *movement*; it is a progression, meaning that it happens in a series of steps, which seldom occur instantaneously. The fact that change involves movement and process suggests that we can expect different things to occur in an expected sequence, even when we can't reasonably expect a given outcome.

Typically, no matter what the change involves, we go through these predictable stages when change takes place in our lives. If we choose to go through the stages in a healthy, purposeful way, we earn the rewards of mastering the challenges of the change. The phases become our stepping-stones to success. We learn to empower ourselves and others so that we can at least remain in control of our reactions to the change, even if we cannot control the change itself. But just as we can learn to empower ourselves and move toward success, we can also learn to be helpless. We can become victims, and our stages become a process that leads us away from happiness. Or, when we have no control over change, we can at least encourage ourselves to find humor in it.

Using humor to deal with misfortune is not a new concept. The Bible says, "A merry heart doeth good like a medicine, but a brittle spirit drieth the bones." More recently, psychological research informs us that human beings want power and authority over our futures. We want to feel that we have a say in how things will go for us, so when we perceive that our actions will make an outcome likely, we feel optimistic and secure. When we don't, we feel insecure. We feel like victims.

Sometimes people stay in a victim's frame of mind after a loss or disappointment. They doubt their capacity to make their lives happen according to their own aspirations, so they wait to be rescued or blessed by good fortune. They start to feel undermined and overwhelmed; and they can become totally immobilized.

However, there are alternatives to these feelings of hopelessness and helplessness. Learning to turn challenges into opportunities is one way to do that, but it won't happen automatically. We need ways to keep our hearts merry or our spirits will become brittle with the perception that we are victims. Humor is a weapon for slaying the dragons and a tool for building cohesion. I learned these lessons in 1996 when I started my doctoral research and moved to Pensacola to join the U.S. Navy's study of the VPOWs.

When the Vietnam Conflict ended in 1973, 566 military prisoners of war returned from captivity in North Vietnam. More than 45 years later, the psychological tests of approximately 300 of these repatriated prisoners show few instances of PTSD. How can this be when other groups in history who have experienced captivity have often shown extreme aftereffects? The answers are varied and complex, but one thing seems clear: The VPOWs had a system that worked, a system for human connection based on control and grounded in the effective use of humor. They created freedom where there was none.

The POWs weren't victims. Their captors certainly *victimized* them, but the POWs never saw themselves as victims, no matter what was done to them. They weren't victims because they took *control* of the few things they could control. They were told when and what and if they could eat; they were told when they could shower, sleep, and use the toilet. They had no say about parts of their lives that people normally take for granted. But they did have control over one thing, and that was their humor perspective. *They* decided what they thought was funny.

Their need for control served as a framework for the POWs who created and maintained a system of strong interpersonal relationships and group affiliation that helped them survive over seven years in captivity and thrive during the years since repatriation. Humor was one of the elements of that system.

Humor has its basis in the individual, but it manifests itself in interpersonal relationships. When responding to what helped them survive, the research respondents described humor from both an intrapersonal and interpersonal perspective. That is, they reported a sense of humor within themselves and the laughter they shared with each other. One participant's observation that, "The larger the group, the more light-hearted things were. The smaller the group, the more intense things were" reflected the comments of many.

As one man stated, "Believe it or not, even under the almost worst of conditions over there, under the right circumstances, we could laugh." They would say, "Well, boy, we're going to look back on this and laugh, but boy, it sure does hurt now." Another participant in my study added,

> The first five months I didn't have a sense of humor. I was having great difficulty finding anything very funny about the situation, and then I discovered by living with other people and the way we interacted, that we eventually started being awfully funny.

He went on to clarify the kind of humor he often found valuable. He remembers, "I lived next to a guy in late '67 who had been beaten very severely." After several days of being beaten on a routine basis, the friend reported he had been threatened that he would have both arms broken if he did not answer the questions the next day. When asked what he intended to do, he replied, "I don't know. I suppose I'll tap with my cast tomorrow." The participant described this as an "almost morbid sense of humor." Another participant called this a type of "in-house humor."

A third participant called this "had to be there humor." In explaining what he meant, he mentioned a specific incident. He had passed a worm of substantial length, so he gave it to the guard, thinking the guard would take it to a doctor and request medical attention for the parasites he obviously had:

> So I handed it to him through the bars in the door on a piece of bamboo stick, and the water girls were on the cell block at the time, and I thought, "Hey, he's going to take it to the doctor," you know, and "I'll get some medicine here." So, he closes the door and he starts chasing the water girls with it, screaming and laughing, and the water cans tipped over.

He further commented that he too remembers mocking the situation to find humor. He mentioned that one of the VPOWs with whom he was communicating used the tap code to communicate that when he gets out and "he fills out his critique sheet," he will tell them "The exercise is real and it lasted too damn long."

According to some VPOWs, the importance and the value of a sense of humor was first and foremost. "Humor allows you to get up every morning and think this isn't the end of the world, so one's sense of humor is pretty critical." One VPOW reported that even after being beaten the men ended up telling jokes to each other despite the miserable conditions of the cell. Some others on the other side of the wall, who had also been beaten, tapped the question, "What's so funny?" The response was, "If you don't have a sense of humor, you shouldn't have joined up." The following examples emerged from Vietnam era stories:

> "It is generally inadvisable to eject directly over the area you just bombed."
> U.S. Air Force Manual

> "Five second fuses only last three seconds."
> Infantry Journal

> "Any ship can be a minesweeper.... Once."
> "If you see a bomb technician running, keep up with him."
> USAF Ammo Troop

> "You've never been lost until you've been lost at Mach 3."
> Paul F. Crickmore (test pilot)

A Navigator's Definition of Latitude & Longitude:
"Latitude is Where We are Lost, & Longitude is
How Long We've been Lost There"
USAF Naviguesser

As the test pilot climbs out of the experimental aircraft,
having torn off the wings and tail in the crash landing,
the crash truck arrives; the rescuer sees a bloodied
pilot and asks, "What happened?" The pilot's reply:
"Beats the sh…t outta me, I just got here myself."

To prevent a disjunction of the self and to find meaning in a situation void of meaning, the VPOWs relied on resources many of them did not know they had. Their internal sense of mirth and humor, their reliance on one another, and their group interactions all combined to create a system for survival. Their humor perspective provided the framework for discovering how to cope with their captivity, and their commitment to one another gives an important perspective about what coping is made of.

The role humor can play in bouncing back from adversity, especially when we are linked to others who will help us laugh, seems critical. At the time of this writing, COVID-19 is terrorizing the world. Yet, every morning on Facebook, I see my friends and family doing what the VPOWs did: they are taking control of their reactions to this tragedy my metaphorically thumbing their noses at it. Here are some of my favorite COVID-19 memes:

- Half of us are going to come out of this quarantine as amazing cooks. The other half will come out with a drinking problem.
- I used to spin that toilet paper like I was on Wheel of Fortune. Now I turn it like I'm cracking a safe.
- I need to practice social distancing from the refrigerator.
- Still haven't decided where to go for Easter—The Living Room or The Bedroom.
- Every few days try your jeans on just to make sure they fit. Pajamas will have you believe all is well in the kingdom.
- Homeschooling is going well. Two students suspended for fighting and one teacher fired for drinking on the job.

- I don't think anyone expected that when we changed the clocks, we'd go from Standard Time to the Twilight Zone.
- This morning I saw a neighbor talking to her cat. It was obvious she thought her cat understood her. I came into my house, told my dog. We laughed a lot.
- Day five of Homeschooling: One of these little monsters called in a bomb threat.
- Day six of Homeschooling: My child just said "I hope I don't have the same teacher next year" … I'm offended.

Vaillant understood the value of a humor perspective when he offered this rule of thumb: "Don't try to think less of yourself but try to think of yourself less."

CONCLUSION

Seldom do people raise their hands and volunteer to suffer adversity. Yet, we know that challenges and threats—unless extreme—often produce growth, not damage. When we learn and develop the coping skills to bounce back from adversity during ordinary times, we face the next danger with more confidence and optimism. Author Herm Albright advised, "A positive attitude may not solve all your problems, but it will annoy enough people to make it worth the effort." When we develop and rely on the four building blocks of resilience, we employ powerful forces for annoying others and for disarming the dragons that we face in our lives. We take control of our response, even when we have lost control of something significant.

The stories of the VPOWs offer numerous examples of men choosing to find purpose in a situation devoid of meaning. For every account of unspeakable atrocity, there are two of heroism and selflessness. For every tear of sadness, there is one of joy. The towering courage of these men, their unwavering commitment to each other, their stalwart sense of purpose, and their indomitable spirit provide lessons in survival, coping, hardiness, and the importance of community. Because they emerged whole, healthy men, theirs is a story of endurance and victory.

NOTES

1   Frankl, V. (1984). *Man's Search for Meaning.* New York, NY: Washington Square Press. P. 86.

2   Mulligan, J. (1981). *The Hanoi Commitment.* Virginia Beach, VA: RIF Marketing. P. 279.

3   Coffee, G. (1990). *Beyond Survival.* Aiea, HI: Coffee Enterprises, Inc. P. 278.

4   Collins, J. (2001). *Good to Great.* New York: Harper Business. P. 85.

5   Hamel, G. and Valikangas, L. (2003). "The Quest for Resilience." *Harvard Business Review.* September. P. 58.

6   Vaillant, G. (2002). *Aging Well.* New York, NY: Hachette Book Group.

9

Disruption Traps

In *Don Quixote*, Cervantes aptly pointed out that "To be lucky at the beginning is everything." I'll take luck at any juncture, but I've noticed that the sooner luck appears, the more likely the success. Like everything else in life, major change initiatives seldom follow a clear, linear path. More often, they're a series of episodes with beginnings, middles, and ends. We tend to focus a great deal of attention on the beginning and remember clearly how things ended, but we often overlook the muddy middle where disruption should occur. This muddy middle also explains why so many people have trouble replicating success. They simply can't remember how they made the major decisions that led to the project's completion, much less its success. So, they repeatedly fall through the same decision-making traps, the most insidious being what I call the "mid-life crisis decision-making trap."

When a team reaches the middle point in a disruption initiative, they can begin to experience some slouching. They've lost the adrenaline rush they had at the start, and the feelings of accomplishment they aspire to feel once they've completed the project loom miles away. Therefore, avoiding the urge to slump and replacing it with a commitment to jump will keep decision makers from falling through the other traps.

In the 1980s, Dr. Connie Gersick began studying how groups fall through these slumping traps. She found inconsistencies and surprising results among the eight project teams. They did not accomplish their work by progressing gradually through a universal series of stages, as traditional group development models had predicted. Instead, the teams proceeded in a pattern of what she called "punctuated equilibrium." That is, the groups Gersick studied experienced periods of prolonged inertia when they didn't accomplish much. Then came a sudden transition. In a concentrated burst of changes, groups dropped old patterns, reengaged, adopted new perspectives, and made dramatic progress.

Punctuated equilibrium suggests that organizations enjoy long periods of stability or equilibrium. Occasionally, leaders interrupt these periods of equilibrium with compact, relatively short periods of qualitative metamorphic change, or revolution. Gersick's findings offer a way to predict the timing of progress in an organization and predictions about how and when groups are likely, or unlikely, to be influenced by their environments.[1]

Her data do more. They present an alternative—a way to avoid the overarching trap of inertia and the comfort of stability. In other words, understanding concepts like punctuated equilibrium and knowing how and why groups have *traditionally* approached works helps, but it doesn't go far enough. To make disruptive decisions and to sustain the innovation that follows, groups must first change their own decision-making *processes* before they can tackle decisions about their projects. Only then can they sidestep the disruptive decision-making traps that spell failure.

THE FAILURE TO FRAME TRAP

Anyone who has taken high school biology knows that syphilis is a bacterial infection usually spread by sexual contact. After the initial painless sore, which people sometimes don't detect, the disease can remain dormant in the body for decades before becoming active again. For centuries this fact confused many. With the discovery of penicillin, early syphilis can now be cured, sometimes with a single shot. However, without treatment, syphilis can severely damage the heart, brain, or other organs, and it can be life-threatening. Syphilis can also be passed from mothers to unborn children.

Because no one had a way of understanding the disease, much less framing the problems caused by the disease, they resorted to other methods—the "blame game" for one. The blame game, whether played in society, organizations, political arenas, or religions has the same rules: People avoid looking for the root cause, take no responsibility for the role they might have played, focus on what others did or didn't do, and engage in duplicity and subterfuge as necessary.

"Where did syphilis originate?" one might ask. It was named for whatever country another country hated most. If you were to ask the Russians, they would say the Polish started it. The Poles blamed the Germans. Germans referred to it as the French disease, and the French criticized the Italians who in turn held the French responsible. The Portuguese condemned the Spanish. No one understood the origins of the disease, so rather than finding it, they accused others of causing it. Of course, we now understand that bacteria, not any group of people, were responsible all along.

People did then what they continue to do: rewrite the facts. Currently, we see massive attempts to revise and revisit history, to blame historical figures who have been dead for centuries for current injustices. This wrong-minded approach to problem-solving distracts people from *current* solutions because the focus remains clearly on the past. Removing a statue of someone who did something offensive in the past, however, does two things. First, it provides a low-hanging-fruit kind of victory. Taking down a statue is far easier than rooting out the cause of *existing* wrongs and allocating time and resources to making things right. Second, it allows decision makers, especially politicians, to bask in the glory of righteousness. They can say to themselves and others, "See? I'm one of the good ones. I worked to right this wrong," even though no one's life improved because of the actions. Innovative thinking and positive disruption can't bring about needed change when people put past decisions on trial instead of focusing on the future.

When an organization faces a significant decision, therefore, senior leaders have the responsibility of *framing* the problem for themselves and others. Like a frame around a picture, this can determine how we view a situation and how we interpret it. Often the frame of a picture is not apparent, but it enhances the artwork it surrounds. It calls attention to the piece of work and separates it from the other objects in the room.

Similarly, in decision-making, a frame creates a mental border that encloses a particular aspect of a situation, to outline its key elements and to create a structure for understanding it. Mental frames help us navigate the complex world so we can avoid solving the wrong problem or solving the right problem in the wrong way. Our personal frames form the lenses through which we view the world. Education, experience, expectations, and biases shape and define our frames, just as the collective perceptions of a group's members will mold theirs.

Because people often react unconsciously to their frame of reference, senior leaders can help a team become aware of the frames they bring to the table. Similarly, when leaders fail to frame the problem or decision effectively and accurately, they miss an important opportunity to influence. Those who effectively innovate and lead major change initiatives realize the importance of the first steps in the decision-making process. Leaders who can structure the discussion about the disruption stimulate their own best thinking and that of others.

To frame, first put the problem or decision into one sentence that does not imply a solution. If it won't fit into one sentence, or frame, there is more than one issue to resolve. In that case, frame each separately. Begin with "The problem is..." or "We need to decide whether..." This simple discipline keeps everyone focused on the objective or strategy before they start discussing alternatives—inside the frame is important to this discussion; outside is not. Also, framing helps reduce mental clutter and achieve agreement about critical areas before moving ahead.

Whether the leader offers the initial frame or someone else does, the group should not automatically accept it. Instead, try to reframe the problem in various ways. Ask, "Is this really the issue?" Force everyone to get to the core of the problem without being distracted by symptoms, indications, causes, or effects.

For example, in many of our public schools dropout rates are high; teacher readiness is low; parents don't get involved; and inadequate funding impedes improvement. While all true, none of these gets to the root of the problem, which is that too many children can't read or do math at grade level. The frame becomes, "The problem is that more than half the children in this school district can't perform at grade level." The group can then agree on the objective: to improve student performance. Starting with any other frames takes the group in a direction that won't get to the heart of the issue, and therefore, won't ultimately solve the problem.

Next, ask questions that test the frame and force new perspectives by encouraging comparisons:

- Are you dissatisfied with _____ or _____?
- How would you compare _____ with what has happened before? What is different?
- When something like this happened before, what worked?
- What resources will we commit to this?
- To what extent are we willing to change the status quo? Structure? Reward system? Reporting relationships?

Frame the issues from different reference points and discover the frames of those who disagree. What biases do people reflect? What agendas might they promote? To circumvent bias, use neutral, concrete language to frame the problem. Challenge assumptions and examine underlying causes. Ask yourself how your thinking might change if your framing changed.

People who understand the power of framing also know its capacity to exert influence. They have learned that establishing the framework within which others will view the decision is tantamount to determining the outcome. Senior leaders have both the right and responsibility to shape outcomes. Even if they can't eradicate all the distortions ingrained in their thinking and that of others, they can build tests like this into the decision-making process and improve the quality of the choices. Effective framing offers one way to do that—sticking to the facts, another.

Facts are our friends. When we face an unfamiliar or complicated decision, verifiable evidence is our most trusted ally, but also the one many senior leaders reject. Instead of steadfastly pushing for definitive information, they settle for the data others choose to present, seek information that corroborates what they already think, and dismiss information that contradicts their biases or previous experience. When guesswork or probabilities guide decisions, we fall into the trap of too little information or the wrong kind of information.

Facts may be our friends, but they are scarce allies. Inferences and judgments, which can be more influential and pervasive, tend to dominate discussions and drive decisions. To the untrained ear, the inference can present itself convincingly as a fact. Inferences represent the conclusion one deduces, sometimes based on observed information, sometimes not. Often inferences have their origin in fact, but a willingness to go beyond definitive data into the sphere of supposition and conjecture separates the fact from the inference.

Similarly, judgments go beyond what one can observe and prove and add an *evaluation* of the information. Judgments offer a perspective—a good/bad coloring of the data. For example, if you were to walk into a room and notice a moose head above the fireplace, you might infer that the owner of the house is a hunter. You may or may not be correct. If you have strong positive or negative feelings about hunting or decorating with animal heads, you might then attach a judgment to your observation. Only one fact is true, however. Either the owner of the house is a hunter, or the owner is not. Perhaps the owner purchased the house with the moose in it.

Maybe the owner's former spouse left it there instead of making it part of the divorce settlement. Several possibilities can explain the evidence. The job of the leader is to separate fact from fantasy.

Personal reactions, or judgments, will vary as well. Senior leaders will subconsciously find themselves drawn to the information that supports their own values and experience. However, if they discipline themselves and their team to gather more data, to check for reliability, and to examine all information with equal rigor, they will take important steps to improving decision-making and removing the leadership blinders that afflict so many.

Scottish scientist Alexander Fleming discovered penicillin in 1928, but people did not begin using it to treat infections until 1942. Imagine all the lives that could have been saved had scientists immediately collaborated to find applications for the new discovery! During World War II, the drug helped reduce the overall number of amputations and deaths because doctors used it to reduce the wait time between when a soldier was wounded and when he was seen by a doctor for surgery or treatment. In the Allied Forces, the average wait time was nearly 14 hours. The longer the wait, the higher the probability the infected area would need an amputation. Administering penicillin immediately vastly reduced the chance that the wound would get infected and increased the survival chances.

THE STATUS QUO TRAP

Welcome as penicillin was for treating wounded soldiers, scientists also discovered its effectiveness in eliminating syphilis. But supplies ran short. Doctors then faced decisions about how to use the wonder drug. They knew administering it immediately to a wounded soldier offered his best chance to recover and avoid amputation. However, even in the best-case scenario, a wounded soldier could not return to combat soon. On the other hand, giving penicillin to a soldier suffering from syphilis would mean he could return to combat immediately. The development of the drug had a measurable impact on the manpower needed to fuel the war effort.

Imagine the debates that ensued! Should we give the drug to a wounded man who served honorably or to a man who engaged in behavior we warned him against? In 1942, nearly 5% of draftees had syphilis, and posters warned "You can't beat the Axis if you get VD," and that venereal disease makes "a sorry ending to a furlough." During World War II, syphilis was the fourth leading cause of death in the U.S., behind only tuberculosis, pneumonia, and cancer. Doctors and leaders had to rely on then-current information, which required putting aside personal reactions and the-way-we've-always-done-things thinking. They couldn't stick with the status quo of administering the new wonder drug only to wounded soldiers and hope to win the war.

Fear of failure, rejection, change, or loss of control—these often-unfounded fears cause decision makers to consider the wrong kinds of information or to rely too heavily on the status quo. According to psychologists, the reason so many people cling to the status quo lies deep within our psyches. In a desire to protect our egos, we resist taking action that may also involve responsibility, blame, and regret. Doing nothing and sticking with the status quo represents a safer course of action. Certainly, the status quo should always be considered a viable option. But adhering to it out of fear will limit options and compromise effective decision-making.

Confusing the risks of a decision with its seriousness also encourages us to stick with conventional thinking. True risk relates to the likelihood of an outcome, while seriousness defines the consequences of that outcome. For instance, the risks associated with flying are statistically small. Driving a car to the airport is the riskiest part of a journey. Yet, because the consequences of a plane crash are gargantuan, fear of flying tops the list of prevalent phobias. Similarly, executive teams frequently adhere to the status quo because of illogical fears. They dread the dire consequences of change, when the likelihood of those consequences remains quite small.

Adherence to the status quo closely aligns with another decision-making trap: the predisposition not to recognize sunk costs. The sunk-cost fallacy describes the tendency to throw good money after bad. Just because we've already spent money or other resources on something doesn't mean we should *continue* spending resources on it. Sometimes the opposite is true, yet because of an illogical attachment to our previous decisions, the more we spend on something, the less we're willing to let it go, and the more we magnify its merits.

Sunk costs represent unrecoverable past expenditures that should not normally be considered when determining whether to continue or abandon a project, because the cost won't be recovered either way. However, to justify past choices, we want to stay the course we once set. Rationally we may realize the sunk costs aren't relevant to current decision-making, but they prey on our logic and lead us to inappropriate choices.

Leaders can steer their teams away from the sunk-cost rationale by creating a safe haven for discussion and admission of mistakes. Sometimes senior leaders inadvertently reinforce the sunk-cost trap by penalizing those who made decisions that didn't work. Instead of admitting the mistake and trying to move on, often the decision maker will prolong a project in a vain attempt to buy time, improve the situation, or avoid detection. Obviously, leaders need to hold their team members accountable, but if others consider the leader draconian or severe, they will hide the truth and soldier-on, making more mistakes instead of cutting their losses.

When considering the status quo, make sure it represents one and only one option. Then ask the key question: "If this weren't the status quo, would we choose this alternative?" We often exaggerate the effort that selecting something else would entail, or we magnify the desirability of staying the course over time, forgetting that the future may well present something different. When we face a multitude of various options, rather than carefully evaluating each, we give into the temptation to stick with the traditional approach.

THE ANCHORING TRAP

A pernicious mental phenomenon related to over-reliance on the status quo is known as anchoring. This *cognitive bias* describes the common human tendency to rely too heavily, or to "anchor," on one piece of information when making decisions. It occurs when people place too much importance on one aspect of an event, causing an error in accurately predicting the feasibility of other options.

Research indicates the mind gives disproportionate weight to the *first* information it receives, to initial impressions, and to preliminary value judgments. Then, as we adjust our thinking to account for other elements of the circumstance, we tend to defer to these original reactions. Once someone sets the anchor, we usually have a bias toward that perception.

Since most people are better at *relative* than absolute or creative thinking, we tend to base estimates and decisions on our known anchors or familiar positions, then adjust decisions relative to this starting point. If I were to ask people if they think the population of a city is more than 100,000, instead of coming up with a number of their own, most will be tempted to use 100,000 as a relative frame of reference.

Another problem associated with anchoring involves decision makers focusing on *notable* differences, excluding less conspicuous but often critical factors that would help in making predictions about achievability or convenience. When the emphasis remains on past events, trends, and numbers these become anchors for forecasting the future. Sometimes these data offer an accurate starting point for making predictions, but too often they lead to misguided conclusions.

For example, on October 16, 1962, President Kennedy faced the central crisis of his presidency and perhaps of the entire Cold War—the Cuban Missile Crisis. To establish a Soviet nuclear presence just 90 miles off the coast of Florida, Premier Khrushchev sent Russian ships carrying nuclear warheads to Cuba. Emboldened by Kennedy's failure at the Bay of Pigs Invasion, Khrushchev told other Soviet officials that Kennedy would do anything to prevent nuclear war, noting "Kennedy doesn't have a strong background, nor generally speaking, does he have the courage to stand up to a serious challenge." He assured Cuba's Che Guevara that "You don't have to worry. There will be no big reaction from the U.S. side."[2]

The Soviets and Cubans underestimated Kennedy. Following an October 14th reconnaissance trip over Cuba, the Strategic Air Command advanced its alert posture to DEFCOM 2, one step short of nuclear war for the first time in history.

Kennedy resisted calls for direct engagement and ordered, instead, a naval blockade of Cuba. The move prevented the Soviet ships from gaining entry to the island and bought time for cooler heads to prevail. On October 22, Kennedy declared that any missile launched from Cuba would warrant a full-scale retaliatory attack by the U.S. against the Soviet Union. On October 24, Russian ships carrying missiles to Cuba turned back, and when Khrushchev agreed on October 28 to withdraw the missiles and dismantle the missile sites, the crisis ended as suddenly as it had begun.

More than a year earlier, however, Kennedy's leadership during the Bay of Pigs invasion had not turned out so well. Historians often blame Kennedy's failed leadership during the Bay of Pigs crisis for the ultimate boldness that caused the missile crisis. Both the Bay of Pigs Invasion and the Cuban Missile Crisis offer examples of disruption at work—the first an example of disruption run amok, the second, disruption fashioned by analytical reasoning, restraint, and up-to-date intelligence.

As mentioned in Chapter 3, the purpose of the Bay of Pigs Invasion had been to touch off a nationwide uprising against Castro, a plan which members of the Eisenhower administration had put into place at the end of their tenure. When Kennedy took office, he abolished Eisenhower's Planning and Operation Coordinating Board, thereby eliminating the checks and balances inherent in Eisenhower's Council.

Kennedy's biggest mistake was voicing his opinion before he heard from his experts. He needed dispassionate data, not echoes of his perceptions. By letting the group know his preference, *and anchoring their thinking*, he doomed the decision. In these kinds of situations—those that require robust examination of all angles—the leader does well to assign a high-powered team member the role of devil's advocate. If Kennedy had assigned this role and then set a second-chance meeting to examine further up-to-the-minute intelligence, he could have saved the lives of hundreds of Cubans, and perhaps, steered the U.S. in a better direction with its relationship with Cuba, which remains strained 60 years after this fiasco. Not only did the offensive fail, it also aggravated already hostile relations between the U.S. and Cuba, intensified international Cold War tensions, and inspired the Soviet Union to install missiles with nuclear warheads in Cuba the following year.

Most historians agree Kennedy and the participants who planned the invasion made some fundamental errors in judgment that they didn't repeat during the missile crisis. While they fell through both the Anchoring Trap and the, next to be considered, Groupthink Trap, in designing the Bay of Pigs Invasion, they avoided both traps as they took control of the Cuban Missile Crisis.

- Perhaps naiveté, hubris, or inexperience caused Kennedy to disregard Eisenhower's plans and the input of dissenting voices during the planning of the Bay of Pigs Invasion. No such overconfidence guided his judgment during the missile crisis.
- Kennedy made the decision to invade Cuba based on the *theory* that the incursion would start a large-scale uprising, a miscalculation that proved later to be erroneous and costly. He more successfully based his conclusions on definitive information during the missile crisis.

- In general, the U.S. created an impression of irresolution in the invasion when it did not show enough aggression in its support of Cuban rebels. Kennedy specifically compromised the U.S. commitment when he refused the air support needed to protect the exiles. Conversely, Kennedy's firmness in his negotiations with Khrushchev during the missile crisis showed the Russian leader that he had been mistaken in his assumptions that Kennedy would not have the courage to stand up to a serious challenge.

- During the Bay of Pigs Invasion planning sessions, a high degree of cohesion and pressure to conform existed among CIA members. They hesitated to challenge one another and intentionally kept dissenting opinions from the President when someone had the nerve to express them. They sidestepped methodical research, planning, checks, and balances, focusing instead on the Machiavellian approach that overthrowing Castro justified any means to an end. Kennedy did not question or uncover their subterfuge and shoddy research until it was too late.

- Kennedy allowed members of the invasion planning group to think affiliation with him and top CIA and military leaders rendered them invulnerable. They shared the illusion that they were insulated because of the secrecy and presidential involvement, so they invented justification for their actions. Kennedy tolerated no such illusions during the missile crisis.

- During the initial discussions of the invasion, Kennedy anchored opinions before he heard from his experts. He needed dispassionate data, but he heard echoes instead, thereby dooming any chance for robust examination of all angles and possibilities.

Kennedy's leadership during his short tenure in the White House offers some of the most profound leadership lessons of modern time. First, the same man led in both situations—one a complete fiasco, the other a disaster averted. He showed us that leaders can learn from mistakes, if they show a willingness to examine what went wrong and commit to a different course of action.

Second, Kennedy illustrated that a failure—even one as large as the Bay of Pigs Invasion—need not define a leader's tenure in the executive chair. Kennedy will be lauded for his pressure under fire, his willingness to compromise with Khrushchev, his resolve, his diplomacy, and his courage. He drew a metaphorical line in the Atlantic and warned of dire consequences if Khrushchev dared cross it, but he also negotiated a peaceful resolution that avoided nuclear war.

Leaders can avoid falling into the anchoring trap by not revealing too much information too soon. Once they give their opinions and shape information, others will tend to defer—to ricochet the ideas they've just heard. When this happens, leaders lose the opportunity to think about the problem from a variety of perspectives.

When leaders carefully think about how they will frame the problem in a dispassionate way, they take important steps to avoid the temptation to become anchored by their ideas and unconscious biases. It's a tricky balance. Effective framing will improve decision-making; anchoring will worsen it. Here's the difference. To frame a decision, leaders might ask their teams the following: "What, if any, marketing efforts should we initiate this year?" Anchoring will occur when you influence the answer: "Should we increase marketing in our Eastern regions by more than 20%?"

Once they introduce the figure of 20%, they have indicated bias that marketing *should* increase by at least that much, and team members will adjust their thinking to consider that. What if the figure should be much higher? The leader would have inadvertently given direct reports implied permission to underperform, and if the company should reduce or eliminate marketing in the Eastern regions, the leader just influenced the team to dismiss those ideas.

To dodge the anchoring trap, remain open-minded, seek the opinions of others, and don't color others' reactions with your own. Frame the issue in a non-evaluative way, refrain from giving opinions too soon, and be alert to language or perspectives that tend to anchor thinking in one arena. Awareness of how anchoring influences each of us defines the first step in sidestepping its effects.

THE GROUPTHINK TRAP

As mentioned in Chapter 3, when we allow inadequate or faulty information to cloud our judgment, we also allow organizational biases to inhibit our ability to discuss risk and failure—and we trap value. When this happens, groups facing uncertain conditions often fall through the

Groupthink Trap. Those who don't remain mindful of the insidious nature of this trap suppress their objections, no matter how valid, and fall in line with others in the group, often to avoid dissension.

High cohesion, a positive group dynamic, creates problems when the group has excessive amounts of it. When groups become too unified, the members, especially the insecure or weak ones, allow loyalty to the group to cloud their ability to make effective determinations. Often these weak participants engage in self-censorship because they perceive that "the group knows better." This, coupled with their fear of rejection and the stronger members exerting direct pressure to conform, discourages the voicing of dissenting ideas and leads to mind guarding.

Mind guarding routinely takes place in these highly cohesive groups. Through subtle or overt pressure, powerful members create an atmosphere of intolerance. The group discourages dissension and prevents the raising of objections. The absence of obvious dissent leads members to conclude that the others concur; they assume everyone agrees; and they engender the *illusion of unanimity.* Mind guarding and high cohesion can further lead to *collective rationalization,* the process through which members invent justification for their actions, causing them to feel they are acting in the best interest of the group. A "safety in numbers" mentality develops that can lead to excessive risk-taking, not positive disruption, when the group feels accountable to no one.

The decision-making that led to the Challenger disaster illustrates how each of these causes of groupthink can lead to a tragic outcome. The Challenger blasted off at an unprecedented low temperature. The day before the disaster, executives at NASA argued about whether the combination of low temperature and O-ring failure would be a problem. The evidence they considered was inconclusive, and more complete data would have pointed to the need to delay the launch.

Cohesion and pressure to conform probably explain two of the main reasons these decision makers fell through the Groupthink Trap. The scientists at NASA and Morton Thiokol felt the pressure of their leaders and the media to find a way to stick to their schedule.

Any one of the causes of groupthink can sabotage decision-making, but in the case of the Challenger, they created a tragic outcome by displaying most of the symptoms. When teams find themselves in the throes of groupthink, they can't always see or understand what's happening. That's why they should take steps to prevent it before it rears its ugly head.

Positive disruption depends on groups preventing groupthink by structuring a systematic approach for evaluating alternatives. The leader should serve as an impartial judge who refrains from expressing a point of view. Groups can further enhance the evaluation process by assigning one of the members the role of *devil's advocate* or *devil's inquisitor.* Inviting outside experts to examine information further contributes to higher caliber decisions.

The chance to rethink a decision occurs when groups set a second-chance meeting. The group can then avoid feeling "under the gun" by agreeing they will make no final decision during the first meeting. Time and distance from the information will allow group members to avoid impulsiveness and quick-fix methodology.

THE COMPLEXITY TRAP

On August 6, 1926, on her second attempt, 19-year-old Gertrude Ederle became the first woman to swim the 21 miles from Dover, England, to Cape Griz-Nez across the English Channel, which separates Great Britain from France.

Ederle entered the icy waters at Cape Gris-Nez in France at 7:08 a.m. She started out that morning in unusually calm waters, but twice that day—at noon and 6 p.m.—squalls impeded her progress. Her coach, T. W. Burgess, urged her to end the swim. Ederle's father and sister, who were riding in the boat along with Burgess, however, encouraged Ederle to stay the course. Ederle's father had promised her a new car at the conclusion of the swim, and for added motivation, he shouted reminders to her that she would receive the roadster *only* if she finished. Ederle persevered through storms and choppy waters, and finally, at 9:04 p.m., after 14 hours and 31 minutes in the water, she reached the English coast, becoming the sixth person and first woman to swim the Channel successfully, battering the previous record by two hours.

Twenty-four years after Ederle's success, Florence Chadwick broke long-distance swimming records for women...*and men.* In 1950, Chadwick crossed the English Channel faster than any other woman in history. A year later, she crossed it again, this time *against* the current, something no other woman had ever done. On July 4, 1952, Chadwick did something else *she'd* never done before.

Setting a different goal for herself and looking for an even greater challenge, Chadwick set her sights on a longer swim, the 26 miles between Catalina Island and the California mainland. On that July 4, she slid into the ice-cold water off Catalina Island and began the long journey toward California's coastline.

As usual, boats holding her support crew flanked her. Some made sure she didn't get hit by other vessels; others ensured sharks stayed away. Shortly after she began the swim, however, Chadwick began to feel nauseous and have trouble breathing. As her crew discovered, one of the boats had been leaking oil. They removed the offending boat, and Chadwick paddled on, stroke after laborious stroke.

Fifteen hours later, another element threatened her attempt at making history: a thick, heavy fog set in on the bay. Chadwick couldn't see her support boats, much less the land ahead of her, and as the minutes passed, the fog grew denser and denser. The water temperatures changed, and the humidity caused her breathing to become more difficult. Chadwick feared she was swimming in circles, and she began to lose hope.

From one of the boats, her mother (and trainer) offered encouragement. Despite her mother's support, all Chadwick could see was a wall of fog. Finally, in desperation, Chadwick did something she'd never done before. She asked her safety crew to pull her into the boat.

Chadwick soon discovered she had stopped swimming less than *one mile* from the California shore. She had swum 25.5 miles, only to quit with a half-mile to go. Later that day, Chadwick explained that she'd quit because she couldn't see the coastline. *She couldn't see her goal, and she lost hope.* Too many things, especially the fog, had complicated her journey and distracted her.

Two months later she tried again. Although she found the fog just as dense that day, she kept going. She finished in 13 hours and 47 minutes, breaking a 27-year-old record by more than two hours and became the first woman ever to complete the swim.

Chadwick had determined a clear way to measure her success: She wanted to swim between Catalina Island and the California coastline. But during her first attempt, she had not developed a plan for dealing with the unexpected fog.

What do these stories of great swimmers with clear goals teach us? First, complexity and clarity seldom march together. Complexity compromises clarity and creates unnecessary distractions. Ederle had a simple goal: swim the English Channel. Some weather conditions interfered with that goal, but she pressed on because she knew what she wanted to achieve. (Her father tempted her with promises of a new car, but I doubt that played a role one way or the other.) Chadwick encountered some unexpected challenges that complicated her journey as well, but she didn't have a plan for sidestepping the traps—at least not the first time. The fog created a barrier to her seeing the goal. Apparently, no one else knew the coast lay a mere mile away either, or that person could have shouted that encouraging news to her. On her second attempt, she anticipated some of the complexities and developed contingency plans for sidestepping them.

Simplicity and lucidity work well together as they encourage decision-makers to embrace "Occam's Razor," a principle attributed to the fourteenth-century English logician and Franciscan friar that states "Entities should not be multiplied unnecessarily." The term "razor" refers to the act of shaving away everything that stands in the way of the simplest explanation, making as few assumptions as possible and eliminating those that make no difference. All things being equal, the simplest solution is best.

Thomas Aquinas recognized the value of simplicity a century earlier when he offered, "If a thing can be done adequately by means of one, it is superfluous to do it by means of several; for we observe that nature does not employ two instruments where one suffices." Albert Einstein added his brilliance to the discussion with his observation that "Theories should be as simple as possible, *but no simpler.*"

The idea that "more is better" and "activity justifies" existence pervades many companies, especially in process-driven departments like human resources. Creating stacks of papers and millions of details does not prove competence; it shows an inability to appreciate Occam's razor. Those who have the capacity to answer a question in a sentence frequently don't seem as dedicated as those who produce a volume of words. More isn't better, but those in power often reward it as though it were. Instead of squandering time on activities that keep people busy but don't improve anything, leaders can prevent themselves from jumping on the complexity bandwagon. They then can help everyone move ahead more quickly on critical issues. When complexity goes unfettered, bureaucracy—the triumph of means over end—follows.

In business, the simplest explanation that covers all the facts offers the best solution, but uncovering it may not be quite so easy. Too often, people lump together the "must haves" with the "wants" and even throw in some "nice to haves." They introduce ways to *execute* a decision before they've made a well-defined decision or even established a goal. They muddy the waters when they deem all aspects of the situation a top priority and skirt around the periphery of the problem instead of cutting to the core of it. They seemingly fail to realize that if everything is a priority, nothing is a priority. Leaders can help teams evade the Complexity Trap by shaving away all but the simplest representation of the issue and reducing labor intensity to concentrate on the problem.

But that's not what Carly Fiorina did. In 1999, when Fiorina assumed the CEO role at Hewlett-Packard (HP), she became the first woman *ever* to lead a Fortune 100 company. In an interview with *Meet The Press*, after the board fired her in 2005, Fiorina spoke frankly about her perceptions of what had gone wrong at HP. Fiorina told Chuck Todd, "It is a leader's job to challenge the status quo, and when you do, you make enemies." Fiorina certainly took risks and caused disruption, but she fell through the Complexity Trap while doing so.

Fiorina had been hired to restore a sense of urgency to HP, which was becoming known more for its printers and cartridges than its innovative products. At first, Fiorina seemed to embrace the founders' philosophy. Then things got complicated.

After the disastrous 2001 merger with Compaq that the founders' children opposed, Fiorina found herself in the midst of a crisis of her own creation. She lacked the skill to run the merged company. (Her successors made it work.) Family members admitted that some shake up had been necessary, but Fiorina didn't take the time to understand what was of value to HP and ended up destroying much of what made the company great over many decades. Board members noted that the company's first value had always been profit and found the deal "all marketing and no substance."

Of all the disruption traps, complexity can be the most pernicious. When leaders like Fiorina fail to zero in on the critical aspects of decisions and put aside the trivial many, they doom themselves to caustic disruption. By their very nature, mergers and acquisitions tend to be messy, complicated affairs. If leaders don't start with a simple deal thesis and *buy-in from stakeholders*, they give up all hope of success.

CONCLUSION

Executives tend to be unaware of the feelings—both positive and negative—that their direct reports have about them. Knowledge of the positive emotions feels good, but ignorance of the negative emotions creates blinders that engender other problems. Unwittingly, leaders condition their people to tell them what they want to hear, even when that differs from what they need to know. Shoot just one messenger, and the other messengers get wind of it. The chances of your hearing bad news, much less conflicting points of view, diminish in direct proportion to the number of messengers in your wake.

"Bounded awareness" describes a phenomenon that occurs when cognitive blinders prevent a person from seeing, seeking, using, or sharing highly relevant, easily accessible, and readily perceivable information during a decision-making process. Bounded awareness also creates disruption traps. It can happen at various points in the decision-making process when decision makers don't gather relevant data, consider critical facts, or understand the relevance of the information they have. It can also happen later when these decision makers don't share information with others, thereby limiting general knowledge.

Often decision makers fail to notice the specific ways in which they reduce their own understanding, and their failure to recognize those limitations can have grave consequences. To make disruptive decisions, leaders must first disrupt their own decision makers processes before they can tackle decisions about their projects. Only then can they sidestep the disruptive decision-making traps and venture into the unknown, often scary muddy waters where positive disruption occurs.

NOTES

1 Gersick, G. (1988). "Time and Transition in Work Teams: Toward a New Model of Group Development." *Academy of Management Journal.* 31.
2 Updegrove, M. (2009). *Baptism by Fire: Eight Presidents Who Took Office in Times of Crisis.* New York: Thomas Dunne Books. P. 185.

10

Leading Disruption

Russian playwright Anton Chekhov once pointed out "Any idiot can face a crisis—it's the day-to-day living that wears you out." He was partially right. The day-to-dayness of running a business wears out the average leader. Facing a crisis and *intentionally* causing disruption requires much more than idiocy. It demands focus, discipline, motivation, resilience, and a whole lot of smarts. Leaders with this combo platter of talents understand that opportunity and disruption often arrive at the party at the same time. Joined at the hip, these two conditions are inextricably linked, meaning a safe path seldom leads to a significant opportunity.

Many leaders think of themselves as innovative. Most of them, however, show up in established markets. Few have committed to introducing genuinely disruptive innovation—the kind that creates entirely new markets and customers. In most industries, growth and success have occurred because leaders with a *Disruptive Mindset* launched them from a platform of disruptive innovation. These leaders have indicated their understanding of one key concept: successful companies with established products *will* get pushed aside unless leaders know how and when to abandon traditional business practices and welcome change.

ALSO-RAN LEADERS

Disruptive leadership starts with a *Disruptive Mindset*, one characterized by strong self-esteem, intellectual horsepower, fortitude, motivation, and resilience. It begins there, but it can't end there. In *Landing in the Executive Chair*, I introduced "F² Leadership" to illustrate the importance

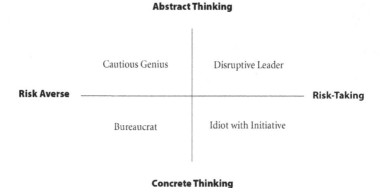

FIGURE 10.1
The Disruptive Leader.

of balancing firmness and fairness. In *The Merger Mindset*, Constance Dierickx and I built on that model when we discussed the "F² Synthesizer" to show the importance of decisiveness under fire and ambiguity tolerance. *The Disruptive Leader* goes another step further to couple risk-taking with abstract thinking (see Figure 10.1).

Risk-Takers enjoy gambling and taking chances. These people willingly expose themselves to situations with uncertain outcomes and enjoy adventures that hint at undefined benefits, even when the person remains unsure about those benefits. Similarly, people standing at slot machines keep putting quarters in the slots, hoping for a defined benefit (money) even when, time after time, the machine fails to pay.

This psychological motivator known as *intermittent reinforcement* involves the delivery of a reward at irregular intervals. People at slot machines don't receive a reward *every* time they perform the slot-feeding behavior nor do the rewards happen according to any regular schedule. Instead, the payoffs come at seemingly random intervals.

Risk-taking leaders often derive gratification from pursuing daring ventures and actively seeking them, even when they can only hope for inconsistent benefits. When they are at their best, we think of these leaders as adventurous, bold, courageous, and enterprising. At their worst, when they don't have the intellect to back up their risk-taking tendencies, we think of them as incautious, thoughtless, foolish, and imprudent.

Risk-taking should not be confused with impulsivity, even though the two often walk hand in hand. *Impulsivity* describes people who tend to act on the spur of the moment without too much deliberation. They speak freely and readily vent their emotions. Hasty and rash, they often display volatility and recklessness—two behaviors that never work well in an organization, even one that welcomes innovation and creativity.

Risk-Averse leaders, on the other hand, tend to be overly cautious about unpredictable situations. They steadfastly refuse to bet, even when benefits appear tangible and likely. They avoid situations of personal risk, even those with great rewards. They don't take chances, regardless of whether the risks are physical, social, monetary, or ethical. We think of these leaders as hesitant, security-minded, and conservative.

Abstract Thinkers possess advanced cognitive abilities. These leaders learn quickly and adeptly apply previous learning to new situations. They grasp ideas, see patterns, and anticipate consequences to decisions. Alert and intelligent, they demonstrate a facility for evaluating options, planning, and problem-solving.

Concrete Thinkers don't. Possessing lower cognitive abilities, concrete-thinking leaders typically fail to grasp the nuances in any problem-solving or decision-making situation. Binary thinkers, they take things literally and interpret situations as "bad" or "good," frequently overlooking intangible benefits to a course of action. More practical than creative, they have trouble conceptualizing anything hypothetical, so they frequently fail at both strategy and innovation. The dullness of concrete thinkers can usually be attributed to low intelligence, but sometimes poor functioning is due to psychopathology.

Risk-averse abstract thinkers appear in many organizations as *Cautious Geniuses*. Years ago I worked with Claire, the general counsel of a large nonprofit medical society, who fit this bill. Obviously, Claire possessed the cognitive abilities that allowed her to graduate from law school and pass the Bar Exam, but no one mistook her for a strategist. She excelled at identifying problems and the dangers of *any* action, but she didn't distinguish between the *probability* of risk and the *seriousness* of consequences. Rather, she found all risk terrifying and threw cold water on most innovative ideas.

Claire aspired to have the role of Executive Director, but she demonstrated the Peter Principle early and became resentful. She thought she deserved more money and prestige, but she played it safe with her career, just as she did with all decisions in her life. Every budget cycle turned into a nail-biting crisis as Claire continually engaged in penny-wise-pound-foolish rationales. Eventually, Claire's fears started to spread throughout the organization and infect others, rendering all the decision makers incapable of creative disruption and dooming the organization to stagnation. I found Claire frustrating to work with. I had been hired to help grow the organization, but she steadfastly planted her feet on the path, blocking progress, evolution, and expansion.

Larry, the Vice President of Human Resources at a large publicly traded company, resembled Claire in his risk-aversion, but he lacked her cognitive abilities. Larry, a *Bureaucrat*, disappeared for decades in the bowels of the corporate headquarters until an M & A deal forced him out of hiding. Until then, Larry had been enamored with his processes and procedures. They didn't really help anything, but they didn't draw attention to themselves either.

Larry leapt from trend to fad, always searching for the next shiny object and most recent bandwagon—Six Sigma, TQM, Lean—anything to help him create the illusion that he was adding value. Larry could have been a poster child for the *Dunning-Kruger Effect*, a cognitive bias that causes people with low ability to overestimate themselves. As the leader of HR, Larry didn't know what he didn't know, and as Charles Darwin pointed out, "Ignorance more frequently begets confidence than does knowledge." Dunning and Kruger took Darwin's idea one step further, suggesting that the less competent people are, the more likely they will be to *unknowingly* exaggerate their own competence, "unknowingly" being the keyword. Larry and those like him simply don't know that they overestimate their own abilities, don't know what they don't know, and have almost no intellectual curiosity that would spur them into the action of seeking innovative ideas.

Larry certainly wasn't a bad guy, and I enjoyed working with him, but that didn't make me blind to his limitations. On the contrary, as the deal progressed, and things got more complicated, as they tend to do in most M & A deals, Larry clung more tenaciously to the status quo. The unfamiliar waters of the deal petrified him. He had spent his career developing systems and protocols that he could pull up on the computer to provide easy answers. He would say things like "He can't do that job because he's an introvert," as though that explained everything we needed to know about an individual.

Before I met them, Claire and Larry had been valued solo performers. They did their jobs, and typically others liked working with them. Problems surfaced, however, when decision makers forced them into the extremely uncomfortable roles of Disruptive Leaders. Neither had the stomach for disruption, preferring to cling tenaciously to all they held dear in their conventional methods, and Larry didn't have the aptitude either.

Contrast Claire and Larry with Randy, the V.P. of Sales at a large Wall Street firm that specialized in computer sales. Randy personified what I call an *Idiot with Initiative*—any company's nightmare. Not one to shy away from risk, Randy understood sales. With apologies to Kenny Rogers, Randy knew when to hold 'em, when to fold 'em, when to walk away, and when to run. Randy could sell circles around anyone else at the firm, but he couldn't lead.

Like a bull in a china closet, Randy lacked sophistication in both his reasoning skills and his behavior. He knew how to read sales situations, even though he routinely showed signs of lacking social astuteness in many other situations, something I haven't seen too often. His "street smarts" allowed him to determine *why* people bought, not just that they did. In a sales situation, he seemed to enjoy the complexities evident in human personalities, motivations, and behaviors, even though he didn't find these same insights especially interesting in normal social discourse. In fact, I found Randy to be obnoxious and dreaded time I'd have to spend with him.

Sometimes these Idiots with Initiative can serve the organization as a dream-come-true in solo-contributor roles, as Randy did, but they truly turn into nightmares when put in a position of leadership. Decision-makers at Randy's firm understood this concept, so they unleashed him on their customers but didn't attempt to have him lead or manage other salespeople, a decision that paid off handsomely. The worst thing about impulsive people like Randy who assume leadership roles is they can do more damage than anyone else. The good news? They have trouble hiding. They are the most visible and apparent people in any organization. To say Randy was thick-skinned doesn't do justice to the typical elephant.

DISRUPTIVE LEADERS

Stark differences exist among Claire, Larry, and Randy—dissimilarities that become even more apparent when comparing them to a *Disruptive Leader*. Unlike their counterparts who find themselves in one of the other quadrants, Disruptive Leaders balance a willingness to embrace risk with clear thinking. These leaders welcome risk because they know they have the intellectual abilities to think things through and figure them out. Like the rhesus monkeys Harry Harlow studied, these leaders feel motivated by a drive that no biological need or reward/punishment scenario can rationalize. Rather, as Harlow explained, these kinds of leaders have a drive to perform a task *for the pleasure of figuring it out.*

For more than 20 years, I have aggregated data from Disruptive Leaders who have reached the level of vice president or higher in my client companies, with companies in construction, manufacturing, health care, financial services, and food represented. On the abstract-thinking measure, the leaders in my study achieved the 81st percentile, which is well *above* average, using managerial norms. On the risk-taking measure, they scored at the 68th percentile, also above average, but on the impulsivity scale, they scored at the 26th percentile, putting them well *below* average—all indicating many of the stereotypes we have about effective leadership simply aren't true. Disruptive Leaders enthusiastically take risks, but they aren't reckless about them.

As exceptional abstract thinkers, these Disruptive Leaders eagerly engage in long-range strategic planning, simultaneously process information from a variety of sources, and deal with multi-dimensional issues. They like to gamble because they feel stimulated by the process of putting together the pieces of a puzzle that no one else has ever put together before. They derive great satisfaction from a strategy that pays, an M & A deal that makes money immediately after the deal closes, and dramatic growth. They take risks not *in spite* of the element of the unknown but *because* of it. We think of these kinds of vanguards as business leaders, but another example springs to mind.

In 1966, rumor suggested Walt Disney had been frozen at the time of his death—cryogenically preserved to await the day when science could revive him and cure his disease. Nothing could have been further from the truth. His body might have betrayed him in 1966, but Disney lives on. He started a fire in the entertainment world that continues to burn decades after his death. *The Saturday Evening Post* hailed him as the "world's most celebrated entertainer and possibly the best known non-political public figure." Arguably, no single figure so dominated American—and indeed even global—popular culture as Walt Disney did. Each year during his life and since his death, millions view a Disney movie, visit his theme parks, watch his television shows, listen to his recordings, buy his products, and read his books. He has held sway in much that has touched our lives, inspired millions of people, and garnered billions of dollars.

We cannot, measure Disney's influence as a film producer, director, screenwriter, voice actor, animator, entrepreneur, and philanthropist by numbers or encomia alone, however. We can only understand it in terms of how profoundly he reshaped and disrupted American culture and consciousness.

The dramatic disruption began in the late 1920s when Disney started reinventing animation, gradually turning it from a novelty that emphasized movement and elasticity into an art form that accentuated character, narrative, and emotion. This reinvention led to him receiving four honorary Academy Awards and 22 Academy Awards from a total of 59 nominations. The accolades included a record four in one year, giving him more awards and nominations than any other individual in history.

How did this award-winning streak happen? By combining his superior abstract reasoning with his penchant for innovation, Disney distinguished himself by becoming one of the first to use television as an entertainment medium, with *Zorro*, *Davy Crockett*, *The Mickey Mouse Club*, and *Walt Disney's Wonderful World of Color* among his most notable works. He also changed the shape of American recreation with his Disneyland parks, reconceptualizing the amusement park as a full imaginative experience—a *theme park*—rather than a series of diversions, shows, or rides.

Most of all, Disney's Disruptive Mindset redefined *pretend* and linked it to innovation. He, more than any other American artist, described the terms of wish fulfillment and demonstrated on a grand scale how fantasy can empower us—how we can learn, in effect, to live within our own illusions and even to transform the world into those illusions. "When You Wish Upon a Star," his television theme song, served as Disney's anthem and guiding principle. He made his own dreams come true and recast the world to be nearer his heart's desire, modeling for us the very essence of entertainment—the promise of a nearly perfect world that conforms to our wishes.

Like most virtuosos, Disney seldom dabbled. Those who knew him grew accustomed to his intensity about that which intrigued him. Largely self-educated, he focused entirely on things that mattered to him—like animation. A man of contradictions, he was both nostalgic with his small-town, flag-waving patriotism, and futuristic in his forward-thinking television programs that helped shape attitudes about technological change.

Disney squeezed every possible profitable squeal and squeak out of such assets as The Three Little Pigs and Mickey Mouse—first by diversifying into a wide variety of activities, then by dovetailing them so all worked to exploit another. He didn't engage in linear thinking—doing something without giving thought to its likely profitability in other areas.

We remember Disney as an entertainment virtuoso whose influence went beyond his initial area of concentration, but we should also think of him as a role model for what leaders in other industries can do if they couple strong abstract thinking with a disposition to take a chance. For instance, Disney advanced film and television, but he *also* encouraged space exploration, urban planning, and historical awareness. In short, he demonstrated how one person can assert his will on the world and wish upon a star—the leader of the club he made for you and me.

Shy, self-deprecating, and somewhat insecure, Disney did not come from greatness. Neither did he attend Ivy League schools. Rather, he grew up in humble surroundings and attended night school to learn to draw. Many lauded him for his successes, but others criticized him.

Some decried Disney during his lifetime; others have waited to disparage him. Views of Disney and his work have changed over the decades, many offering polarizing opinions, calling him a paradigm of American imperialism and intolerance, a debaser of culture. Others have blasted him for his sentimentality and stubborn optimism, citing his "feel-good" rewrite of American history. His highly praised, very popular films have also drawn harsh criticism from those who called his works "flawed" in a plethora of ways. Some said *Snow White* was badly drawn; *Fantasia* had lurches into bathos; *Alice in Wonderland* didn't remain true to Lewis Carroll; and *Peter Pan* vulgarized a children's classic.

In every industry, Disruptive Leaders set themselves apart from the pack, thereby taking up arms against a sea of trouble *and* suffering the slings and arrows of outrageous fortune. By dint of their success, Disruptive Leaders become targets for the competition and the jealous in and outside the organization. As Bishop Fulton Sheen once said, "Jealousy is the tribute mediocrity pays to genius." Part of the risk-taking associated with disruption is the risk that former fans become critics, but the most successful leaders don't allow these distractions to derail them.

They keep a laser-like focus on goals and strategy. Typically fast-paced and results-oriented, they dutifully and religiously ask for input from trusted advisors and those on their teams but then courageously own the innovative decisions—accepting both blame and accolades gracefully. They actively seek counsel while also eschewing unsolicited advice. Grounded and systematic, these leaders make mistakes, but they learn from them and move on, putting guilt and worry aside. They consider experience a valuable teacher but, like success, they know it can have its limitations.

SUCCESS IS A LOUSY TEACHER

Bill Gates once admitted that success seduces smart people into thinking they can't lose. Billy Joel told us "You're not the only one who's made mistakes, but they're the only things you can truly call your own." Most of my clients tell me they have learned more from accidents than anything they learned in school, but many don't realize they give disproportionate weight to *experience*, especially successful experience.

Experience entices leaders into thinking that just because something worked *before* that it will work again. Or just because something worked in another organization or at another time in history or in another industry, the same approach will work here and now. This wrong-minded thinking explains more than one failed effort and the reason most M & A deals don't deliver on the deal thesis.

Accident investigations steadfastly look for cause with investigators constantly asking, "Why did this happen?" Deconstructing success doesn't happen in the same way. Decision makers routinely ask, "*What* happened?" ignoring the processes and details that would explain *why* it happened. Similarly, most leadership teams fail to unwaveringly dedicate the requisite time and attention to the "near misses" in their world. They too often focus on outcomes, ignoring process.

Outcome bias describes the tendency to overvalue the *results* of a decision and undervalue its quality. It arises when leaders base a decision on the outcome of previous events, without regard to *how* the past events developed. Outcome bias causes us to ignore analysis of factors that lead to a previous event and to *de-emphasize* the events preceding the outcome while overemphasizing the results.

We shouldn't confuse outcome bias with *hindsight bias*. Hindsight bias, also known as the *I-knew-it-all-along* phenomenon, refers to the common tendency to perceive past events as having been more predictable than they actually were. Unlike hindsight bias, outcome bias does not involve the distortion of past events. While not identical, both biases tempt us to twist our thinking, and both compromise our abilities to make successful decisions.

Gamblers frequently fall prey to outcome bias. Even though casinos statistically come out ahead far more regularly than players do, many gamblers use anecdotal "evidence" from themselves, friends, and acquaintances to justify their continuing to play. This outcome bias, that continuing to play could result in winning a large amount of money, prevents the gambler from leaving the casino.

A focus on outcomes also tempts us to evaluate a decision on its merits, even if its soundness may vary. If everything turns out well, we're more likely to think that the decision was not just effective but also morally sound. Gamblers justify their behavior when they win, often thinking, "That was the right thing to do" but seldom admitting "That was dumb" when they lose. A positive outcome can lead us to stick with a questionable strategy, and a bad outcome can cause us to change or discard a strategy that may still be worthwhile.

Our attention to outcomes, and disregard for the processes that created them, make solutions seem more valuable than preventive actions. In most organizations, most of the time, the person who spots the fire and puts it out will receive accolades that escape the person who prevented the problem in the first place.

In *Fooled by Randomness*, Nassim Nicholas Taleb offered another perspective: the value of luck. He investigated the roles that opacity, luck, uncertainty, probability, human error, and risk play in the decision-making world we don't understand—influencing how we perceive and deal with happenstance.

Taleb noted the most recognizable character of all remains unnamed— the lucky fool who happens to be in the right place at the right time—the one who embodies the "survival of the least fit." Such individuals attract devoted followers who believe in their guru's insights and methods even though no one can replicate the windfall Lady Luck delivers.

The author questioned whether we can distinguish the fortunate charlatan from the genuine visionary. Must we always try to uncover nonexistent messages in random events? It may be impossible to guard ourselves against the vagaries of the goddess Fortuna, he noted, but we can be a little better prepared.[1]

In their article, "Fooled by Experience," authors Emre Soyer and Robin Hogarth pointed out that "failures can share some of the same traits as successes" and "if certain factors always lead to failure, we won't be able to discover them by studying only success." They also cautioned against ignoring fiascos because doing so masks failure rates. Concealing the prevalence of failures makes it more difficult for us to learn from them. Instead, we are fooled into thinking that we have more control over success than we actually do.[2]

Success is inherently unpredictable. Both successes and general experience betray us because we view them through multiple filters that distort reality, limiting our capacity to figure out what is *currently* going on around us. We think of successful experiences as our guides for the future, reliable sources of insight upon which we can bank. The facts tell a different story.

In *Factfullness* Swedish author Hans Rosling recalled his first emergency as a new doctor. Paramedics rolled in a stretcher bearing a man in green overalls and a camouflage life jacket. This military pilot couldn't control the twitching in his arms and legs; his color was bad; and copious amounts of blood had already covered the floor. The inexperienced Swedish doctor panicked as he realized he couldn't figure out how to get the "Soviet fighter pilot" out of his "spacesuit." Rosling grabbed a pair of plastic pliers to cut through the fabric, all the while addressing the terrified patient in Russian, trying to reassure him. Rosling assumed the Soviet Union had launched an attack on Sweden and that World War III had begun. Fear paralyzed him.

Just as he began to cut, the head nurse came back from lunch and snatched the plaster pliers from his hand, hissing, "Don't shred it. That's an air force 'G suit' and it costs more than 10,000 Swedish kronor. And can you please step off the life jacket. You're standing on the color cartridge and it is making the whole floor red." She then addressed the pilot in Swedish and explained that he had been in icy waters for 23 minutes, which was causing his shivering, bluish color, and unintelligible speech.

Dr. Rosling was a young doctor handling his first emergency and facing his fears of a third world war. He didn't see what he wanted to see. He saw what he feared seeing. Abstract thinking can prove difficult in the best of times, but as Dr. Rosling demonstrated, it can become almost impossible when we're scared. When fear occupies our minds, facts don't stand a chance.

That day, Rosling didn't have any experience in handling that kind of emergency, so he had neither success nor failure from which to draw. But then he did. The author noted he would forever remember his complete misjudgment. Everything was backwards: the Russian was Swedish; the "war" was a routine mission; the epileptic seizure was cooling; and a color ampule inside the life jacket had caused the "blood."[3]

We don't have to get things backwards, but we often do. As Dr. Rosling indicated, we can base our decision on a clearer world view if we force ourselves to examine outcomes *and* the processes that led to them. Too often leaders search for *confirming* evidence when they really could use *contradictory* data. Failing to seek disconfirming information often leads to yet another predisposition, *confirmation bias*. This tendency to search for, interpret, favor, and recall facts that support previously held beliefs causes us to remember information selectively and to interpret it in a subjective way. Leaders who want to make better decisions can learn from success, failures, and near misses *only* if they reward those who naysay, bring bad news, disagree, and challenge assumptions. And it wouldn't hurt to have people in the chain of command like Dr. Rosling's head nurse.

Risk-taking based on experience makes the crucial assumption that the future will resemble the past. It may or may not. Leaders who want to avoid the classroom of the lousy teacher must take steps to prevent enrolling in that curriculum. Studying both failures and accidents, deconstructing success, and rewarding problem-prevention can lead to creative disruption, not just disturbance. As Hillel Einhorn, one of the fathers of behavioral decision theory asked, "If we believe we can learn from experience, can we also learn that we can't?"

CREATING A DISRUPTIVE CULTURE

What happens when new and fast-improving innovations create opportunities to unleash trapped sources of revenue—some of them long trapped by company, market, and industry inefficiencies? This is the question Disruptive Leaders seek to answer. "Trapped value" and "value trap" should not be confused, however.

A *value trap* is a stock or other investment that appears to be cheaply priced because it has been trading at low valuation metrics for an extended time. A value trap attracts investors who want a bargain. These investments seem inexpensive relative to historical valuation multiples or the prevailing market multiple. The danger of a value trap presents itself when the stock continues to languish or drop further after an investor buys into the company.

Trapped value, mentioned in Chapter 3, describes the *potential* revenue that has become imprisoned in the organizations because of their existing business models and capabilities. In companies, trapped value exists when leaders can see an economic opportunity, but they feel helpless to act upon it because of their concrete thinking and an over-reliance on outdated processes and procedures. A shake-up needs to happen to unleash the company's potential, but traditional business models and rigidity interfere with growth and improvement.

In any industry, trapped value occurs when companies fail to come together to grow the market, seed new innovations, or accelerate infrastructure improvements. For example, retailers once realized they could un-trap value in the industry by joining with other retailers to form shopping malls, and in the 1980s, shopping malls sprang up like mushrooms throughout the U.S. That worked well for a few decades.

Now, many shopping malls have closed or turned into ghost towns as online shopping, and distribution channels have changed and improved. When the 2020 COVID-19 pandemic hit, and people self-isolated, shopping online became the "go to" method of acquiring products. Many people even chose to have their groceries delivered, a service only the elderly and home-bound had previously used.

The pace of change made possible by technology and the speed with which that change can happen have begun to diverge. As the gap between *potential* and *actual* value creation widens, more of the good that new technologies can do becomes hidden. This creates a *trapped value gap.* A corporate culture that doesn't encourage innovation and technological advancements doesn't hold out much hope for keeping up with the competition.

People bat around the word "culture" as though it were a conversational shuttlecock. When an individual, merger, or organization fails, culture takes the blame. We use the word arbitrarily, citing it to explain why things don't change, won't change, or can't change. Culture has become a subtle yet powerful driver that leaders strive—often futilely—to influence.

Traditionally we defined corporate culture as the pattern of shared assumptions that a group adopted to explain "the way we do things around here." When something worked well, members of the organization taught the behavior to new people. Through this process, newcomers found out what others thought and felt about issues that touched the organization. These perceptions helped coordinate activity tacitly—without communicating too much or thinking too often. "Culture" offered a simple defense for just about everything but explained almost nothing important, like its ties to business results.

We developed codes, jargon, symbols, rules, and norms to share our assumptions about what would and should happen and raised each new litter of novices to embrace both the artifacts and the assumptions. Explaining culture started as a well-intended attempt to understand how humans work together, and then it gradually morphed into a La Brea Tar Pit where good intentions go to die amid all the dinosaurs and fossilized specimens of organizational decisions. There's a better way—a way to build a purpose-driven culture.

Blaming recent failed mergers and acquisitions on incompatible cultures hastened the formation of wrong-minded thinking. People should have criticized faulty decision-making and good old-fashioned bad judgment instead. Soon, *patterns* of bad judgment—those things that don't work but that people are loathe to change because "we've always done that"—emerged. The culture trap took the form of anti-innovation, anti-risk, and eventually, anti-success.

Conventionally we defined corporate culture in vast, sweeping generalizations. Now we understand that only some *parts* of a given organizational culture are relevant to organizational transformation. What are they? And why do leaders continue to fail to do the things that would overcome resistance to change?

Ineffective leadership seldom happens because of rusty management skills. Similarly, organizational disasters usually don't occur because of a flawed culture—at least not the traditional definition of culture. They happen when leaders do violence to good sense.

Decades ago Peter Drucker advised that if you want something new, you have to stop doing something old. Yet the facts continue to indicate that 80% of the time companies don't lose sales to the competition; they lose sales to the status quo, a formidable enemy within. Why? Often leaders don't understand that they themselves don't truly understand culture and its relevant elements.

Transformation begins with the leaders' core beliefs. These values reflect those perceptions that leaders consider "correct." Over time, the group learns that certain beliefs work to reduce indecision and doubt in critical areas of the organization's functioning. As leaders continue to embrace these beliefs, and the beliefs continue to work, they gradually transform into an articulated set of *espoused* values, norms, and rules of behavior. Eventually, these beliefs become embodied in an ideology or organizational philosophy that serves as a guide for dealing with ambiguity, risk, and innovation.

For many companies, becoming the *disruptor* rather than the *disturbed* depends on a fundamental shift that turns disruption into opportunity and releases trapped value. A paradox appears. As the Baby Boomers head into retirement, we realize the number one challenge facing organizations today is hiring Disruptive Leaders before the competition does. Leaders know they must attract new hires with a competitive salary without going outside of their current operational funding. Who are these Disruptive Leaders and how do companies hire them, when they don't have readily available financial resources to offer better compensation?

One way involves releasing trapped dollars the company currently spends on inefficient or missing processes in the firm's operations that don't seem to make it to the bottom line. When leaders have the courage to apply innovation by reinventing ways to work more effectively, they make things better, not just different. Similarly, when they shift their focus from the day-to-day operations to financially led initiatives, they foster innovation and tie financial outcomes to increased profitability. When they also commit to a fast-paced approach to mastering leading-edge technologies and making use of existing technologies, they better meet customers' changing needs. These Disruptive Leaders concentrate on the *top*-line growth and not the *bottom*-line cost savings and budget cuts.

Hiring those who have the potential to develop into Disruptive Leaders offers another alternative. Hiring Disruptive Leaders and creating a culture of disruption doesn't happen overnight, but it has to begin with a dedication from senior leaders and board members to top-grade talent.

Future Disruptive Leaders distinguish themselves and exemplify the E^5 *Star Performer Model*: Ethics, Expertise, Excellence, Enterprise, and Experience. They force people to take them seriously. They don't raise the bar—they set it for everyone else. They serve as gold standards of what people should strive to be and attain. If you were to scour the world, you'd be hard-pressed to find people who do their jobs better. You wouldn't hesitate to hire them again, and you'd be crushed if you found out they wanted to leave.

FIGURE 10.2
E^5 Star Performer Model.

Because they excel at abstract thinking, others look to these luminaries for guidance and example. Often, peers consider them edgy and contrarian, but they seldom ignore them. Disruptive Leaders chafe at too much supervision or tight controls—fortunately, they need neither. They constantly search for the new horizon and welcome the unforeseen challenge (see Figure 10.2).

Disruptive Leaders push the edge of the envelope with their fast-paced, take-no-prisoners orientation, but they never compromise *ethics* along the way. They understand that living well demands *doing* something right, not just *being* in a state of integrity. They know honesty isn't some kind of raincoat they should don when weather conditions indicate they must. Instead, they wear integrity like a cape that protects them against slips into a jungle mentality.

Expertise describes the raw data of the Disruptive Leader's talent. It encompasses intelligence, talent, and knowledge. Most leaders can learn to follow a protocol or set of procedures. Give them a plan, and they can execute it. They know how to run fast, but Disruptive Leaders have the expertise to know which race to run.

Excellence has to do with consistency of performance. Although required, expertise won't be enough to lead disruption. Even when people possess world-class talent, they must practice and hone their skills routinely and religiously.

Talent—the natural ability or aptitude to do something well—stands firmly at the foundation of excellence, but *awareness* of the talent must occur too. Unknown potential does little good if we leave it in the realm of the unidentified. Passion, knowledge, and discipline spur Disruptive Leaders to organize their lives so they can apply their excellence.

Enterprise relates to setting the bar for self and others. No one I've worked with in the C-suite succeeds without a strong achievement drive. The willingness to work hard and a high-energy-go-getter attitude define "enterprising." A competitive spirit, a "can-do" attitude, and reliability further aid in helping the Disruptive Leader embrace challenges and overcome obstacles.

I describe *experience* as the yesterdays that define the tomorrows. When I advise clients on hiring and promotion decisions, a recurring challenge I face involves helping them evaluate experience. Most senior leaders tend to overvalue it, especially when a person has "just what we need" in terms of previous employment and industry experience. When clients ask me to help them spot potential Disruptive Leaders, I look at experience differently.

I don't want to see a resumé that chronicles 15 years of experience when 10 of those years really amounted to one year, ten times. Similarly, a long list of jobs that showed no advancement in decision-making abilities or development of skills doesn't impress me.

It should come as no surprise that high-growth companies invest more aggressively than other companies in both people and technology. As the world recovers from a pandemic and continues to be disturbed by natural and man-made disasters, it is critical for organizations to invest in advances that can create entirely new markets. As technology advances at a rapid pace, the gap widens between high-growth disruptors and the disturbed.

INSPIRING CREATIVE DISRUPTION

Joseph Schumpeter, one of the most influential economists of the early twentieth century, popularized the term "creative destruction" to warn against the repetitive process of recycling the old into new. According to him, the economy is a living organism that constantly grows and adapts to changes. Over the years, Schumpeter has garnered much attention and worldwide approval and has helped mankind advance through the economic world.

Creative destruction involves the dismantling of long-standing practices to make way for innovation. Schumpeter originally advocated creative destruction in manufacturing processes that increase productivity and described creative destruction as the "process of industrial mutation that incessantly revolutionizes the economic structure from within, incessantly destroying the old one, incessantly creating a new one." Recently we have started to use the term in other industries, especially those that rely heavily on technology.

Creative destruction describes the *deliberate* dismantling of established processes that make way for improved methods of production. In the 1940s, Schumpeter and those like him coined the term to describe what they saw in things like Henry Ford's assembly line. Then, people started to use it to explain "new" disruptive technologies such as the railroads. Now we use it when we talk about things like the internet. Netflix offers a modern example of creative destruction at work. Having overthrown disc rental and traditional media industries, we have become accustomed to the "Netflix effect" and being "Netflixed." The theory of creative destruction assumes that long-standing arrangements and assumptions must be destroyed to free up resources and energy to be deployed for innovation.

The word "destruction" implies the process inevitably results in losers and winners. Vanguards like Steve Jobs predictably create disequilibrium and highlight new profit opportunities. Those committed to older technology find themselves stranded. So, while Henry Ford's assembly lines revolutionized the automobile industry, they also forced many laborers out of work, and completely erased companies that made buggy whips. Similarly, the internet displaced many bank tellers, travel agents, and small retail businesses. Uber and other ride-share companies have put many taxicab drivers out of work.

The winners have been just as numerous, however. As Schumpeter noted, the evolutionary process rewards improvements and innovations and punishes less efficient ways of organizing resources. Clearly, companies need decision makers who can anticipate consequences and take *prudent* risks. But how do we spot them? And how do we rise above the stereotypes that tell us what makes a leader great? The simple answer is "data."

One stereotype suggests great leaders are cautious, analytical Vulcans who dispassionately review data, putting aside emotions, concentrating entirely on logic. These Dr. Spock CEOs concentrate on science but become paralyzed by disruptive decisions and stick with the knitting too much and too often. They also don't remain in the executive chair too long, unless they own the company. We might think of some of them as *Cautious Geniuses*, but I have met very few of them in my career. Certainly, Disruptive Leaders carefully evaluate risk, but they don't strive to eliminate it.

Another stereotype tells us fleet-footed Road Runners run the corporate world, always outsmarting the cunning coyotes of the competition. Legends imply these leaders act impulsively and decisively, always willing to pull the trigger and shoot from the hip on the next deal that will put the Acme company out of business.

The facts tell a different story. In my original longitudinal study, I found those who excel in the hot seat resemble Goldilocks. These successful leaders carefully gather data and know when things are "just right."

Renowned author William Arthur Ward once noted, "The pessimist complains about the wind; the optimist expects it to change; the realist adjusts the sails." Disruptive Leaders spend their careers adjusting sails while remaining optimistic, constantly looking for solutions that are "just right," not perfect. They know when to take risks, not because they have mastered rescues but because they have prevented the need for them. The day-to-day decision-making and risk-taking involved in running a business with a growth strategy doesn't wear them out. It energizes them.

CONCLUSION

Disruptive Leaders understand that disruption doesn't *cause* growth. It's the other way around. Growth causes disruption. They know the only way a company can grow is by launching new growth business when their core units are strong. They realize that they can't bet the company's tomorrow on today's reliable customers and trusty strategy. They create engines capable of generating new business opportunities over and over again. They find profitable customers who are not satisfied by existing offerings of competitors. They place bets continuously and religiously because doing so is the only way to get a few to pay off. And while growth can prove complicated, it isn't as random and failure fraught as it sometimes appears. Most of all, they have the confidence and capacity to lay the groundwork for healthy growth.

NOTES

1 Taleb, N. (2004). *Fooled by Randomness: The Hidden Role of Chance in Life and in the Markets*. New York, NY: Random House.
2 Soyer, E. and Hogarth, R. (2015). "Fooled by Experience." *Harvard Business Review*. May. P. 74.
3 Rosling, H. (2008). *Factfullness*. New York, NY: Flatiron Books. PP. 102–103.

Index

Printed in the United States
by Baker & Taylor Publisher Services